Reaching
BEYOND
Your Pulpit

Reaching
BEYOND
Your Pulpit

Edited by FRANK S. MEAD

FLEMING H. REVELL COMPANY

COPYRIGHT © MCMLXII BY FLEMING H. REVELL COMPANY
Westwood, New Jersey

Library of Congress Catalog Card Number: 62-10733

Printed in the United States of America

1.1

Preface

Is there a preacher anywhere who has not been asked by some parishioner, "Where can I get that sermon in print?" Or, "I wish ten thousand people had been here this morning, to hear that!" Breathes there the preacher with soul so dead who never to himself hath said, "I wish I could reach out into this community, to people who never come to church"? That deep longing to spread the Word is at once the passion and the despair of the good and concerned preacher.

There are ways of doing it; thanks to the hunger of men for something more than bread, highly effective media of communication have been developing, in recent years, in five areas: radio and TV, books, magazines, the newspaper and, generally, in the field of the minister's public relations in the growing community, which make it possible if not imperative for the alert minister to reach a larger and larger audience. Only the lazy or the uninformed or unconcerned ignore them. But few know how to go about it! Many are called to this larger ministry; few are chosen to write or broadcast mainly because they are unfamiliar with the demands and techniques of publishing and broadcasting media. That is just too bad: Billy Graham, using all five media, reaches with one sermon more listeners than all the evangelists of the past century in their combined lifetimes.

It can be done. The preacher *can* "communicate"; he can reach far beyond his pulpit. This book is designed to help him do just that, to show him how. Authorities in these five fields, men with records of success, describe the pitfalls, procedures and profits (spiritual!) of this new great adventure into the media of mass communication. They cover everything from original

5

ideas, through the development of contacts with key people in the arts and industries to be employed and the selection and arrangements of materials, to the final act of broadcast or publication.

For any errors of omission or commission, we offer our apologies. There are probably some, for in this field methods and manners and requirements change swiftly, from day to day. This book is not offered as the last word, but only as a word from which to start reaching for that elusive but highly desirable larger congregation.

Frank S. Mead
Editor

Contents

Reaching
BEYOND
Your Pulpit

1

The Medium of the Press

HILEY H. WARD

ONCE UPON A time there were three pastors who set out to build houses of words for all to see.

One built his house of straw, and called a newspaperman to come to see his house.

His house of words began:

"A very unique event will be experienced Sunday. From three until six o'clock, in the social room of the Ford auditorium, members and friends of the Avenue Church [real name of church withheld] will pause again to observe the founding of the church forty-two years ago."

He added some more words:

"The occasion will be the church's annual Easter Tea. Avenue Church was organized by a small group of former Alabama Congregationalists who were led by the late Charles Hall and Mrs. Amy L. Johnson."

And:

"The small band of members met at first in homes. . . . The Easter Tea, one of the highlights of Avenue's year of activities, is ably chaired this year by Mrs. George Carpenter. . . ."

But the big, bad newspaperman huffed and puffed. Who cares about a forty-second founders' tea? There are thousands of others like it, and pastoral anniversaries, too. A golden jubilee or centennial, yes, but not a forty-second anniversary.

He huffed and puffed and away went the house of words. It missed the chasm of the wastebasket. When the big bad editor picked it up, he decided, since he was on his feet, he would take it to the box for the women's department and then have a cup of coffee before facing the rest of the mail.

After the coffee, the religion editor looked at a whole village of new houses of words.

There was one little pastor who had built his house of sticks.

All the construction materials were there—Who? What? Where? When? Why? How?—important questions to answer in writing a news story. And there was significance, and novelty, and a telephone number to check the source. It was a story about a family with a new way of worshiping in the home. You check with the husband, and he arranges for you to come out with a photographer to develop and expand the story. But then as you get into the story, some snags begin to develop, things like "the suburban papers all used it two weeks ago" or "your Sunday magazine will have a big feature on it in a few weeks," or "it had one six months ago," or, after you get out to the subject's home, with a photographer, the wife, with whom you did not check, says "I told Henry, and Pastor Jones knew, too, our family doesn't want any publicity; thank you for coming all the way out here. My husband should have known better. After all, I told him."

And so the mean religion editor begins to huff and puff and sees a pretty good-looking house of sticks come falling down, too.

Now a third pastor was seeking to get something into the newspaper.

"Good morning. This is Pastor Nelson. How are you today?"

"Fine, thank you."

"Say, Alphonso is going to be making a guest appearance in our church this week," says Pastor Nelson. "It's going to be one of our biggest days. All of our people, of course, know him. . . ."

You, not willing to broadcast your ignorance, listen, picturing Alphonso as perhaps as one of the many foreign dignitaries —most likely from south of the border—that show up as speakers in a big city.

Then, at last . . . you ask:

"Just who is Alphonso?"

The pastor chuckles, expressing his delight having taken you in good humor into his scheme. "Alphonso is a duck. He sleeps in my study in a box. We're taking him to Bible school tomorrow morning."

You laugh, too. Your ears pick up, even though you know this pastor, just new in town, already has had more publicity than some others get in a lifetime.

A pastor's pet duck.

There's a fission that goes on when an idea strikes—most ministers would abhor the idea of studying beside a loudmouth duck—so ministers would be curious to read this piece about the honorable Dr. Clarence T. R. Nelson and his parsonage pet, Alphonso; the story would be a natural with kids, too; it might interest the average layman, the factory worker, to find a white-necked duck looking at him from the church page instead of a white-collar man shaking hands with the mayor, sitting at a table with other celebrities, turning a shovel of earth, or pointing to the latest drawing of a new education building.

Yet one can't fill up a religion page with a duck and let the hard news go by. Nor could one give too much prominence to a duck at the expense of the local clergy, many of whom are destined never to have their picture or a write-up about them on the church page.

The solution: Use the duck story, but drop it in prominence. So Alphonso the duck made the church page.

There he was, his head up, one webbed foot lifted proudly. He was close-up because the photographer was lying on the sidewalk and Alphonso, undaunted as he was, had walked right to the camera. Behind him were a host of happy Negro boys in fancy shirts and girls with big ribbons on their pigtails, followed by their white-collar pastor, all gawking at their idol on the way to Bible school.

Above Alphonso's picture on that Saturday's religion page were the major religion stories of the day: an interview with a Brazilian bishop, visiting his former parish in Detroit, telling what the newly released encyclical of Pope John XXIII, "Mater et Magistra," meant to Latins—attached to it on the right was comment by a leading Presbyterian mission executive and how the encyclical related to Cuba, and on the left, an article "Politicians Like Pope's Encyclical" featuring comments of Wayne County (Detroit-area) Democratic and Republican chairmen interpreting the encyclical and its bearing on politics. These all surrounding Alphonso, featured in a picture and an article describing "A Duck's Big Day" at church:

Alphonso, the four-month-old duck that sleeps in a parson's study, never had it so good.

Some of the religious refinement that surrounds his box in the room with the Rev. Dr. Clarence T. R. Nelson, pastor of Scott Memorial Methodist Church, rubbed off on his slick feathers.

As a reward, he was told he could go to vacation Bible school at the Scott Church, 609 Kirby.

There would be scores of youngsters there.

In bed at 7 P.M., he was up with a quack at the sound of the first running water in the sink in the morning.

He jumped into the tub, flapped his wings happily, then let out gleeful, but terribly lonesome quacks.

He pulled down the towel that is all his own.

He got out and stood still as Mrs. Nelson dried him.

Alphonso was adopted by the Nelsons when their twenty-two-year-old daughter Lydia left for a position in Washington in May with the Division of Temperance and General Welfare of The Methodist Church. Alphonso had been a wide-eyed duckling just out of the shell when he was given to Lydia as an Easter gift by her sister's husband.

Alphonso came down Kirby, quacking, his head up, smelling of Cologne, and looking for the attention he craved.

He found it in a horde of boys and girls admiring each little gesture.

He liked especially Ray Payne and Gregory Smith, two eleven-year-olds, who defended the merits of a duck against those who thought dogs were better.

He heard Ray, who has a fox terrier, say, "Alphonso is easier to train and you can make him come to you."

He approved of Gregory, a boxer owner, who sang his praises because "A duck minds easier and I like to see when he's down in the water to get food."

Alphonso visited the departments of the vacation Bible school and disrupted them to nearly pandemonium with his intelligent quacks.

He even said the opening remarks on a telephone call back to the Free Press.

But he became anxious to get back to the familiar water spray and the puddles at the parsonage at Hague and Brush.

He felt himself shaking a bit and panting, nervously. A few loud quacks brought some favorite pellets. Then he rested his long white neck on "Grandma" Nelson and let his head hang over her shoulder and his bill closed contentedly.

"Nice baby," she said.

Alphonso had held up well, but he was ready now to admit that he was no more than he really was—a four-month-old baby.

Needless to say, Pastor Nelson would not have had his picture in the paper, nor his vacation Bible school mentioned, had it not been for Alphonso.

With all the huffing and puffing of the big, bad editor, the idea was strong enough to stand upon its own—in spite of many possible objections that could be raised later (there were none) by denominational headquarters and local church publicity committees more anxious than Alphonso to promote a cause.

But how many pastors eat, sleep and study with a duck?

A dog maybe.

Or a cat. But not a duck.

Well, take a cat, then. How can a pastor with an ordinary pet around get into the news?

In the small country church—and many big ones, too—there may be a cat on its ninth life who has proudly seen to it for years that a rat or mouse does not interrupt a church service. Only once has this author seen a healthy rat, undaunted, come out and make his appearance by a pulpit, then slowly traipse off, leaving the giggles of children behind and a pastor wondering what he said or what was wrong with the way he looked. This scene is uncommon only because there are a lot of stalwart tabbies that stalk the church halls across the nation successfully keeping out little varmints that do not belong there.

Such a church cat reaching a milestone in its life was featured in the *Chicago Daily News* article, "FUR FLIES IN GLEN ELLYN: Church Board Spat Begat by Its Cat," by Emery Hutchison, with a blurb, "Curious Tabby Paces Corridor While Meeting Ponders Its Fate":

The board meeting of the First Methodist Church of Glen Ellyn was torn assunder Tuesday night.

All had been harmony among the fifty members attending during discussions of plans for the church's $350,000 addition.

Then Ridgely A. McCrary, a board member who is a buyer for Marshall Field and Co., dropped a bombshell with this question:

Should Tabby, the church cat, be retired?

McCrary so moved and was seconded and the fight was on.

Someone asked why retirement?

He was reminded that Tabby had a bad habit of wandering out to the pulpit during addresses by guests—recently Dr. Charles Ray Goff of the Chicago Temple, for example.

One board member suggested that this merely enlivened the speeches.

But he was harshly reminded that the merriment of the congregation should not be weighed against a guest's embarrassment.

During all of this the brown and white cat, whose innumerable kittens are in homes scattered all over the Glen Ellyn area, could be seen through an open door, pacing the church corridor.

A proposal was made that the cat be caged during guest appearances.

It failed when no one volunteered to be chairman of the committee for caging the cat.

Clay Steele, secretary-treasurer of Hart, Schaffner and Marx, then started a heated discussion with a request for a definition of "retirement."

It finally was decided that this did not mean execution, but rather the finding of a suitable home.

The Rev. James D. McKelvey, the pastor, ventured the opinion that they might not have a right to retire Tabby.

"Last summer I received an anonymous gift of $10 for an operation on Tabby to reduce the population of kittens around the church," he recalled. This operation was performed.

"Does anyone," he asked, "know that donor, who might claim ownership?"

Yes, several board members admitted, they knew the donor, but each was true to his trust. They refused to identify him.

Clarence McGee, assistant treasurer of Quaker Oats, wondered aloud: "Isn't a cat a church necessity for keeping mice out of the organ?"

Mrs. Vera Erickson scoffed at this. "Hasn't anyone ever heard of mouse-traps?" she asked.

Someone said that this was all a waste of time, since the durable cat had survived several previous church boards.

But at last it was put to a vote.

A chorus of "Ayes" from those in favor of retirement was matched by an equal chorus of "Noes" from those opposed.

The Rev. Mr. McKelvey then asked for a show of hands. The count of those voting was 18 to 19.

The verdict was retirement.

So the word was going around in Glen Ellyn Wednesday: Does anybody want to take over the custody of the old church cat?

There are clergymen who say such stories waste space in the newspapers. But do animal stories really waste space?

For one thing, what better story could be put in its place? A substitute might be the latest crime story, or should a substitute be a straight announcement about a church program or tea? People might read the crime story, depending on the crime and criminal. But who would read about the church tea? The group which sends it in, the small handful out of a community of 2,000,000 and 600,000 subscribers? Maybe, but even that readership is doubtful, for they know what the story says, and are really concerned with just the fact that it got in.

Which does more for the reader?

The tea story emphasizes that the church strives to be a club, that it is concerned with its own, that it is far removed from life.

A story about a cat or duck, to take extreme examples, shows there is some spontaneity, some life, some concern with the little things, some sincerity and love on the part of the church.

If a pastor can tell as much about his church in a newspaper as the duck and cat stories tell, surely he could expect to tell no more. He has already told a lot. The dogma and creeds and formulas essential to the way his church sees things can come in his own sermon in the sanctuary or, if he is using a medium that is not his own, such as a secular newspaper, through paid advertising.

Yet a church does not have to depend on advertising as the only door to a newspaper. There is news space in most newspapers, really thousands of acres of white space that go begging for good news.

The good soil is there in a newspaper and can produce towering results.

A newspaper is a fertile place for seed such as the gospel, the best news ever.

Yet what appears to be good seed does not always bear fruit in good soil. There are conditions and problems, such as too excessive planting, not enough weeding or cultivating, bad weather conditions or timing that permit a lot of newspaper space to go unused by churchmen.

How can you improve the harvest?

First, you must separate the good seed—the good idea— from the bad, in planting. Your newspaper can help you, but you should do this yourself, if your church is to be right in there with the other leading producers of news copy. The minister needs to recognize the chaff from the wheat germ or life of a story.

What is some of the good seed that ministers try to plant in the newspapers? What is some of the bad seed?

Knowing the difference between a good idea and a bad idea is a big step to success in newspapering.

So let's first look at some of the good ideas.

Some good ideas are shown in a sampling of comments gleaned from a questionnaire sent to representative religion writers whose job it is to accept or reject news ideas from the clergy.

"A group of clergymen conducted a survey of county schools to see how many children were eating breakfast and found that many did not have a meal until supper time," said Alan Moore of the Huntsville (Alabama) *Times,* citing the best offering he's had from clergymen. "They then got various churches to adopt a school to furnish extra food. It fell flat, but it was a good idea."

Mrs. Hilda M. Spence, church editor of the Chattanooga *News–Free Press* liked it when "a Lutheran pastor here called and told me that a medical doctor in his congregation was going to New Guinea as a missionary. He had five children and he and his wife were as thrilled as could be that they had been accepted to serve in that part of the world. The doctor had a fine practice here, which didn't seem to concern him."

"A tip from a minister that one of the local churches has an altar and stained-glass windows more than 500 years old" was one of the best that religion staff writer J. O. (Jimmy) Mizell of the Tuscaloosa (Louisiana) *News* had.

Other ideas which religion writers liked best from ministers include:

"Feature on how local pastors feel about being called Reverend"—Mrs. Alice Wade, Coffeyville (Kansas) *Journal*.

"Feature on Calix Society, Catholic organization for alcoholics"—Judy Hierseman, Green Bay (Wisconsin) *Press-Gazette*.

"Motivation survey made by a Corpus Christi foundation"—Melvin Steakley, Houston *Chronicle*.

"A feature about a minister who started a youth group among colored children in his church's neighborhood"—Miss Freddie Boyle, Camden (New Jersey) *Courier-Post*.

"Local story connected with Father Mario Borelli and his activities with Italian orphans. This incidentally was received from a divinity student, who was Borelli's aide"—Dan Hunt, Greenwich (Connecticut) *Time*.

"Story of a minister's wife who works unselfishly in behalf of the blind. Particularly interesting because she is colored"—Bess Watson, Indianapolis *News*.

"Christian Family Week program of First Baptist Church, Birmingham, Alabama" (feature included series of pictures illustrating ways to worship and pray at home)—Claude Keathley, Birmingham *News*.

"Rural minister who tipped me off that a white family in his congregation was inviting a Negro family of eleven to spend a week's vacation on the family farm"—Willmar Thorkelson, Minneapolis *Star and Tribune.*

"Tip that snake-handling church was operating here"— James A. Haught, Charleston (West Virginia) *Gazette.*

Some of the best ideas from clergymen, according to two religion writers, come indirectly when ministers made themselves and their resources available to the brain-picking of the press.

"Most of my best stories I have developed from chance remarks rather than from direct suggestions from a minister," says Margaret A. Vance, religion editor for the Newark (New Jersey) *News.* "These have included a series on ministry to migrant farm workers, several on articles that are rare and/or historically significant (a number of New Jersey churches are more than 300 years old), unusual services, such as a Reformed Church restoring the old type of communion service for Maundy Thursday of having the congregation sit around the Holy Table, a custom which the consistory had voted one hundred years previously to change; unusual hobbies of clergymen; how a clergyman uses classic cars as his trademark and introduction to teenagers to transport them to Sunday school and vacation Bible classes, etc."

Pittsburgh *Press* church editor Robert W. Schwartz has one minister who goes so far as to select a good personality, interviews him, and sends a transcription of the interview to the church editor. Such was the case with the minister's organist who doubles also as a medical student and intern. "The minister interviewed the organist after one of the rehearsals, had a tape recording made and then had a secretary record the interview for me. It was not a case of his doing my work. He knew a good personality story when he saw one, and he helped to get it into print. I, of course, wrote the story."

The best idea simply resulted from a relationship—a give and take among clergy and press.

Not all religion writers can report a "best" idea for a news story from a clergyman.

Some say, concerning their clergymen's ideas: "none outstanding"; "none that has been outstanding"; "it is almost rare that a minister offers any sort of article"; "ministers do not provide us with stories. We have to go and get them, or suggest stories to them"; "can't remember—in my experience, they rarely come up with anything except the obvious"; "frankly, I rely far more upon church bulletins and publications and my general knowledge of what's going on than upon ministers for story ideas."

The ministers of the gospel, of the good news, are also bearers of bad seed or news when seeking newspaper space.

Knowing what the weeds are, as well as examples of productive ideas, can be very important in avoiding a bad harvest as one seeks to bring forth a good crop.

The religion writers also tell the worst ideas ministers have submitted to them.

Ideas such as—

"Printing sermons en toto."

"Derogatory articles on Catholics and John F. Kennedy."

"The monotonous repetition of submitting only sermon subjects, who takes part in an installation or ordination and routine facts about church anniversaries or church dedication service."

"Story on vacation Bible school."

"Pictures of visiting choirs."

"Picture idea of young people 'picketing' the church on Sunday against nonattenders at training union. It cheapened the church."

"Printing sermon topics."

"Running pictures of themselves with every article about their church."

"The suggestion that we publish a story or series of stories dealing with the doctrine or policy of a certain church."

Others say:

"Too many ministers bother to deliver in person piddling announcements about a bazaar, dinner, or even a guest choir or speaker."

"Founder of 'Salvation Air Force' (lives nearby) wanted us

to sponsor a contest to design him a plane (with propellers like crosses) to drop church leaflets on the communists."

"One minister in this area has brought in his own picture to run with a story when he is having a guest speaker."

"Most want to use the newspaper as a pulpit and are too wordy."

"I particularly dislike ideas related to revivals, church socials and the routine."

A Texas reporter says she dislikes "any idea in which the clergyman tries to plug his own prejudices, particularly at the expense of another denomination or conviction. The 'What a wonderful, fund-raising, soul-raising, hot-shot *I* am' type." A California religion writer says he can't put his finger on the worst idea for there are "many poor ideas—nearly all dealing with promotion of their church and/or themselves."

For a minister to crack the newspaper with good stories—stories that are competitively good and do not merely seep in because they are filling a big vacuum, the minister first should re-think the orientation of his faith and attitude.

He needs to reappraise his capacity for creativity, imagination, and tolerance for what is new. He needs to see if he is just a part of a machine, or if he is still a person, reacting sensitively to the persons and stimuli around him.

He must first feel, think, be informed or study to know the facts, have some imagination or creativity, and care—before his ideas can interest others. The early church fathers such as Tertullian or Augustine might have put it this way: *Patior, cogitor, studeo, imaginor, custodio—ut scribam.*

An unthinking, impassionate, routine "person"—the nondescript man who is at home in every situation—is not going to have much to say of either importance or interest to the larger community.

Rate yourself, first as to your role as a human being. Your newspaper consciousness depends on it.

Ask yourself questions such as:

Did I laugh at others today?

—Did I laugh at myself?

Did I write a letter to a church member today?

—Did I write to a non-church member?

Have I bought a meal for a colleague?

—Have I bought one for a bum on the street?

How much time did I pray?

—How much of my time can be traced to working explicitly for that which I prayed—such as peace of the world, overcoming a jealousy, reasoning with a difficult elder or deacon?

Did I speak to a group today?

—Did I speak to an individual in an isolated location?

Did I teach something?

—Did I learn something?

The list could go on. If you were able to check every other question "yes"—the ones beginning with a dash—you probably rate high in the basic quality for being creative—that of having feeling, essential to newspapering as it is to the arts and pastoral communication.

You could sharpen your consciousness of good ideas by isolating in thought one aspect of your church program. Brainstorm all the possible variations concerning it as far as news interest is concerned. Remember, in brainstorming no idea is too absurd. In news, no idea is really too absurd either.

A little Danish church in Detroit was announcing that it was forming its choir for the season, and needed recruits. A routine type of announcement. But in the announcement letter, the director of music quoted some authority to the effect that singing made ladies look younger.

The idea to look younger has universal appeal.

So the director of music was contacted to see if he thought he could support his statement—he did, and with the help of our photographer, was able to demonstrate that some of the ladies very advanced in years through the use of their facial muscles singing in his church were preserving their youth beyond expectation. This was only one of many variations possible with a choir story.

Strive for ten variations on the theme of your routine events.

You could submit these "variation" ideas with your usual announcement—and once in a while, you might find what is normally a paragraph notation might end up a picture feature on the front page.

There are other ways of sharpening up the creative process and producing exciting, discriminating ideas.

When an idea presents itself, entertain the opposite. Then resolve the conflict through some process of reasoning. For even with common ideas such as God is good, entertain the opposite, such as God is *not* good. Then begin to line up mentally the arguments on both sides. You may begin to think of examples in your parish illustrating that God is good—there may be a former skeptic who learned through some crisis in his life that God really is good; or maybe there is someone who through tragedy could never again entertain the idea of God being good, but through the love of a Christian in the parish applying his faith in action toward him, came to realize this. The former could make a very good feature, the latter a news story, especially reported at the time of action and decision.

The Bible has a lot of good news stories. Turn to it for ideas. Take most any page and seek modern counterparts. For instance, consider Adam and Eve—does this not start you thinking about the conflicts of the modern man and wife and the way good things of their lives, the modern luxuries, conflict with worship of God—specific instances of temptation and how it was overcome has possibilities recounted in a newspaper. Consider these topics, too, in their modern parallels in getting ideas for newswriting: interesting military personnel in your congregation, the modern-day counterpart of Joshua, the pious militarist; the reluctant servant type, the Samuel or Gideon, as seen in modern persons who have hesitated to serve. (At the last Methodist Jurisdiction Conference I attended several men declined becoming bishop—why these men decline, why they accept, on any level of church life, the questions answered preferably at the time of decision, might be a good news feature); Rahab, the harlot turned good, or the burlesque queen now a model mother or Sunday-school teacher—and if one is hard to find who is leading a changed life, the minister could debate the local representative of sin, and a transcript could be used; Job, the great sufferer, seen in his modern counterparts; the Psalmist on the hillside, versus the modern camp story.

The New Testament stories that Jesus told would make wonderful news stories retold with modern counterparts. In place of the Prodigal Son, a juvenile delinquent returned home; a Good Samaritan, a modern philanthropist; Lazarus, the beggar, today the Skid Row bum, hungry and suffering in a well-fed community; parable of the tares, those who are sowing indecent literature in the community, etc.; the mustard seed, the little event growing to spectacular proportions, the $10 a year given by a multitude of businessmen to build great churches; the parables of the pounds and the paying of the laborers, counterparts today would be novel ways for Christian investment and a Christian's concern or lack of concern in wage disputes; Jesus' taking money from the mouth of the fish to pay taxes and a modern Christian's attitude toward taxes. There are germs for great news stories today hidden in every corner of the Bible.

The Bible, too, has some good advice on how to write the news story and to get it into the paper.

Go through a chapter like I Corinthians 14 and underline ideas that apply to communication, especially writing in or for a secular newspaper. Mark ideas such as "Follow after charity," "he that speaketh in an unknown tongue speaketh not unto men," "if the trumpet give an uncertain sound, who shall prepare himself to the battle?," "except ye utter by the tongue words easy to be understood, how shall it be known what is spoken? for ye shall speak into the air," "there are . . . so many kinds of voices in the world, and none of them is without signification," "seek that ye may excel to the edifying of the church," "let him that speaketh in an unknown tongue pray that he may interpret," "I had rather speak five words with my understanding . . . than ten thousand words in an unknown tongue," "let all things be done unto edifying," "if there be no interpreter, let him keep silence," "God is not the author of confusion," "let all things be done decently and in order."

For the minister who aspires to newspaper communication there are good mottos in the Bible. My favorite is Proverbs 24:33, 34: "Yet a little sleep, a little slumber, a little folding of the hands to sleep: So shall thy poverty come as one that travelleth; and thy want as an armed man." There's Psalm 116:6, "The Lord preserveth the simple: I was brought low, and he helped me"; Matthew 5:37: "Let your communication be, Yea, yea; Nay, nay"; and there is a lot of good advice in I Timothy, such as turn aside from "vain jangling" (1:6).

Read over these verses dealing with communication in the Bible and you have a pretty good documentary on how to write—simply, sincerely, without rancor, accurately and thoroughly, and with significance.

When writing simply, "yea, yea" and "nay, nay" without vain janglings, words like "unique, recent, noted (speaker), famous, special, dedicated, contemporary, traditional, highlights, featured, unusual," should never be used, although there are exceptions. Use only words that mean something. "A noted preacher, Don Jones, who has had an unique ministry as an evangelist in Terre Haute, will be the featured speaker at the 9 A.M. and 10 A.M. Sunday morning services at First Baptist Church" becomes "Evangelist Don Jones, of Terre Haute, will speak 9 and 10 A.M. at First Baptist Church. . . ."

There is no substitute for simplicity and hard facts. You can never be too specific. Give the addresses for all places mentioned in your news item; spell out first names, John Jones, never J. Jones; give the time and place of the meeting; include titles but never give a title unless you know for sure that the person has it. Also always identify a picture. Two out of three pictures I receive at the religion desk have no identification whatsoever. Most of these must be destroyed. The religion writer does not like to hazard a guess as to who is who.

In groundbreaking stories or dedication stories, don't refer to the new structure as the "first unit" of "new contemporary church," but rather a "$250,000 sanctuary or social hall to be used for worship." All churches are contemporary, but not all are tentlike with roofs descending to the ground, or modern Gothic, or shaped like a fish.

Put in the corner of a release to your newspaper: your name, your title at church, address of church, and where you may be reached by phone. The phone number helps the religion editor to check a fact, if he wishes, or to expand the story; but if the release is not complete, the phone number will not save it. With all things being equal—and most church announcements are —and with more received than can be used, the religion writer will tend to give first preference to the release that is complete and answers specifically all the five W's.

You can test your newswriting by listening to police reports on the radio, then writing up what happened. Or better still, and easier, tune into a TV documentary, such as a rescue story or an account of some major political event, and write it up the way you feel it should go into a newspaper. The President's speech, which is not fully reported until after it is given, is a good subject to work with. Pick out the highlights, as you see it, and write it up as a news story. Check the way you wrote it with the wire service and other newspaper accounts the next day. Or, if you go to a big church rally—such as a Reformation Day rally or national convention meeting—and you know that the press is there, go back and write it up the way you feel it should go in the paper. Then seek out the respective papers in your community and compare your version with those whose trade is to report religious events.

The matter of style is a complex thing and is best left to the textbooks, classrooms—and experience. For the minister is not expected to stylize or make copy "sing," of course, unless he is a columnist or a professional newsman himself. Generally all copy is rewritten to fit a particular newspaper style. Even with the smaller papers, the weeklies, a straight presentation of facts is the way the article would go in anyway, so a straightforward article, for all practical purposes, is the best way to write it.

Generally, the best rules for all-purpose newspaper writing are these:

1. Pick out the most unusual or interesting aspect to lead out with. This should answer some of the five W's. The rest of the five W's should be answered as soon as possible.

2. Tell the story as though you were writing a letter to a friend.

3. Avoid words ending with "ness," "tion" etc.—in other words, stay with the one-syllable Anglo-Saxon word as much as possible, "God" for "deity," "see" instead of "perceive," "said" instead of "relate" or "retort," "ask" instead of "interrogate," etc.

4. Keep your wits about you, and since we all make mistakes, it's good to check back over what you write. A time span whenever possible (and this is rare in daily reporting) between writing and submission is helpful by permitting a check back over and polishing up of a communication.

For example, had a clergyman checked back over the announcement in a church bulletin received by a Kansas religion writer, he might have wanted to change the wording of the item in the bulletin which said "Pastor Smith left Monday morning with a carload of young ladies to attend Girls' Camp. Let's all pray for the girls this week."

In a Lutheran newspaper before me is a small headline on page nine which says "Martini Members Laid to Rest." The lead is no better, for it starts out: "Two members of Martini congregation fell asleep in Jesus the same morning. . . ." Now, presumably Martini is the name of a church, but a check back over the headline and lead might have given preference to playing up "church" instead of "Martini," which many do not associate with a church.

Or take this notation in a state-wide Methodist weekly: "Rev. John Jones [the name is changed from the original] for seven years superintendent of the Methodist Home for the Aged at Main City [substitute for real city], was found dead of a gunshot wound in one of the buildings at the Home on Oct. 18.

Mr. Jones had been in ill health for some time. He had just completed his annual report. . . ." A check back over the item might have led the editor to want to eliminate the implication that the annual report was so shocking that it was more than the poor man could take.

Charles A. Stevens, religion editor of the Flint (Michigan) *Journal*, provided that extra look himself that saved a local minister from embarrassment. The minister had come into his office near the end of World War II, and was talking about his forthcoming sermon. "It was Mother's Day," says Stevens, "and he had unwittingly chosen the topic 'Battle of the Bulge.' I explained it was Mother's Day, not Motherhood Day, and he got the point." The exclamation "Read your copy!" followed by a string of swear words . . . every reporter some time in his career probably has heard from a city or assistant city editor. Ministers, read your copy, too.

Poor spelling is bad manners, like dripping a chocolate ice-cream cone over your neighbor's new white rug. But that is what many ministers do with their words, dripping sloppily over the newspaper white space and letting their host clean it up. "Some of the copy submitted by local clergy," says a religion editor in a California resort town rather harshly, "indicative of low calibre intelligence and/or education is frequently side-splitting."

When you expect space in a newspaper, as you might expect to occupy so many square inches of floor space and so many cubic inches of air at a social occasion, you've got to be there when you are expected. Yet tardiness, or indifference to a time-schedule or deadlines, is the biggest problem which ministers have in their relationship with newsmen. This concerns not only clergymen, but their appointed representatives. How often does the religion writer on a metropolitan daily, with the next edition only a few hours away, hear concerning a real live story a sincere but nonchalant "I'll get it to you in the mail. You should have it in a few days."

Never mail a story to a newspaper, unless it is an announcement of the event well in advance. If the story is about an event that is happening, such as a resolution from a conference, an important vote of the church, etc., telephone your newspaper directly or bring it in.

The tendency among clergymen (and other professional and dedicated people, too) is that the better the story is—especially if they recognize that they have a good story, such as a multi-million-dollar building project or some comment on a nasty civic affair—to clothe their actions in secrecy, pick out a special day of issue, usually the fat Sunday paper, that they want it in and tell the newspaper when to print it.

When a group operates with this approach, it ends up with getting a lot less space than both you and your religion editor counted on. I can think how this backfired in many instances. In one case, I agreed with the first part, to sit on the story, as long as everybody else did, too, and they would give me first crack at it. What they meant was that I would get the first shot at it in the city. So this story, a building project outstate that would serve the immediate area, was covered by a local small-town newspaper. What they didn't realize was that small-town papers, too, have stringers for the wire services. Immediately there was a short story on the wires which crept into the papers. When Sunday came nobody was interested in a feature. The news was old. You can't sit on a good story any more than you can hide a city under a bushel. For when you hold up a story for just the right psychological moment and for the maximum amount of space, you are in fact choking it to death and when word of its existence finally leaks out, you will have a pretty life-less thing before the public.

Remember the newsman on the religion beat is working against the clock, not the calendar. His sources, too, must have a sense of urgency, if religious news is to be successful in competing with other news.

A leisurely trip to the post office is no substitute for a rip-tearing race down the expressway to the city room of a newspaper. You've got to move, like the young Catholic priest in

the news area of Judy Hierseman, religion editor of the Green
Bay (Wisconsin) *Press-Gazette*. "In a letter to clergy concerning
a special church page during Holy Week," says Miss Hiersemen,
"I stressed, as usual, the deadline time and the fact that I would
not accept any copy after 2 P.M. on Monday. As the Catholic
Church chimes started ringing 2 P.M., the door burst open and
a harried young priest dashed, full-speed, through the door.
After catching his breath, he reported he had just run three
blocks to get his Easter copy to me by 2 P.M. and was outside the
door when the chimes started ringing. He then raced three
flights up the stairs to meet the deadline!"

Religion editors differ as to how they want the usual run of
news submitted to them, news such as announcements of guest
speakers, groundbreakings, festivals, ordination and installation
rites, farewell parties, etc.

A few religion writers will take information on church meetings over the phone. But most religion writers resent being
asked to record a church announcement phoned in—his desk
is confused already, and somebody in a hurry may be sitting in
the chair next to him with a long release and pictures concerning a major story, a photographer may be humped nervously
on his desk, dropping hot ashes from a cigarette or cigar on his
papers, reminding him that he is due, or past due, for an interview out in the big city some place. You just don't have time
to take the announcements over the phone. So most religion
writers prefer and insist the announcements come in well in
advance so they can be routed to the proper folder or stack.
This has another advantage—accuracy. In case he's challenged
as to the day and time of a meeting, or the precise spelling of a
two-inch Polish name, he can look back on a written announcement and point to what was sent in by writing.

When the story involves the whole community—really involves it, such as tearing down a historic site or announcing a
new prelate for the area—the story should be sent in duplicate
to the religion writer and the city editor, noting on the copy
that the story is being sent both places. The religion writer

might be out of the office for a day or a week, and this alerts the staff to the story. This way the story, if important, will be guaranteed coverage in the absence of the person normally assigned to that beat.

Keep in mind these Ten Commandments:

1. Thou shalt have no other newspapers before me—that is, newspapers like to have the same release date, and too, a date that favors that particular paper. Of course, papers like exclusive stories. One man—a professional public relations man at that—called with a "unique" scheme, so he thought, that of having each paper carry the same story, staggered several months apart. That is OK, but who wants to be the second or third paper in the arrangement? If you want to be in all of the papers, give all of them your story at the same time with a fair release date for all.

2. Thou shalt not make unto thee any images as to how you think your story should look in the paper. Then you won't be disappointed if it doesn't come out the way you expected.

3. Do not take God's name in vain. Do not expect every club meeting and social activity in God's name to get on the religion page. There may be far more important religious news.

4. Remember your deadlines, and keep them holy.

5. Honor your father and mother, your senior pastors and retired deaconesses and missionaries, but remember, too, the children and the young adults whose faith in action make very fresh reading. Remember, too, that Jesus said, "Who is my father and my mother and my brethren—it is he that doeth the will of him that sent me." Those are the people we should hear about, too.

6. Thou shalt not kill anything. Send us a calendar, let us know what you are doing—briefly, of course—and leave the slaughter to the religion writer and the copy desk. Too many of us practice birth control and infanticide when it comes to ideas. We revert back to the old days, and discourage the birth of new ideas.

7. Thou shalt not commit adultery. This could mean for the

minister with news ambition to stay with his own business of the gospel: he will be much better off newswise.

8. Thou shalt not steal or borrow the ideas of somebody else and expect good coverage. Many have held Every Member Canvasses or Sector Project drives before you and many have built colonial churches before you.

9. Thou shalt not bear false witness. Be positive. Don't try to expose the Jehovah's Witnesses, the Roman Catholics, the World Council of Churches, the Jews, for as Jesus says, "the beam is in your own eye, too."

10. Thou shalt not covet your fellow ministers' publicity. If one man is getting all of the publicity, maybe he deserves it, maybe he doesn't. "Do not sound a trumpet before thee, as the hypocrites do in the synagogues and in the streets that they may have glory of men. Verily, I say unto you, They have their reward." Publicity for publicity's sake is not a chief goal of the church. Some of the most Christian churches in your city, I am sure, are those who get no publicity at all. The main thing is to be a doer of the word, seek ye *first* the kingdom, and sometimes the other things, such as publicity, are added.

Besides being a good idea man and writing intelligent and effective releases about the life of the church, there are other ways a minister can enter directly, and personally, into the newspaper. His comments on current events, his sermon, a letter to the editor, and a regular column are four ways.

Every so often—sometimes as many as two or three times in the same month—there are local, international and ecclesiastical crises on which the opinion of a clergyman is welcomed by a newspaper.

If you have some idea about the latest rise or fall of a dictator, satellites, moon shots, boycotts, Freedom Riders and variations of the sit-ins, the Congo, Berlin, Brazil, Red China, birth control, the Peace Corps, alcoholic beverages, gambling, race relations, the election of a Pope, the visit of an archbishop of Canterbury or Orthodox figure to the Pope—at the time these are front page news, do not hesitate to call your religion editor and volunteer comment. Chances are he is wishing you and ten others—any ten—could give some quick, intelligent comment, and he is flipping through the directory now looking for clergymen who can be reached readily. On current event comments you need to be prompt, very prompt. You may want to say that you are preaching on the subject Sunday. The religion writer may ask for an advance or he may suggest simply that you have a copy of your sermon or an excerpt in his hands by such and such a time and he will use it in the Sunday or Monday paper.

The sermon is news, or can be news. According to Dick Wager of the Cleveland *Plain Dealer,* who led a discussion at the Religious Newswriters Association meeting in Buffalo in 1961 on coverage of sermons, a good sermon can no more be ignored than any other Sunday morning event, such as a fire or accident. But he warned of preachers "who think they rate a story simply because they 'spout on communism.'"

The *Free Press,* initiating three columns of religion on its second front page every Monday, in addition to Saturday pages and other church coverage, may have excerpts in some form from as many as a half dozen sermons each Monday. The two lead articles in the "Weekend in Religion" column most normally include an interview with a leading religious leader in town for the weekend and a report of a religious service, with a few lines from the sermon. At the bottom of the page and sometimes at the top, depending on significance, is a third feature, excerpts from three sermons, with pictures, from Protestant, Catholic and Jewish clergymen who gave the sermons over the weekend.

When Alan Shepard was hurled into space, the sermon the following Sunday, which was Ascension Sunday, by a Lutheran pastor was "Jesus, the First Astronaut," and what the pastor said was news. A leading Negro pastor assailed the police department, a Jewish rabbi described how he saw Americans behave abroad, a Catholic priest argued that God had rights which might supersede the rights of man, a conservative Protestant declared there was a literal hell in answer to a previous sermon by another clergyman a week earlier that said there was no eternal, literal hell—these were all provocative and relevant sermon approaches that rated headlines in the sermon quotation section of the Monday religion column.

"A minister's subject matter should descend from the clouds," says Dan Hunt, of the Greenwich (Connecticut) *Time*. "Christian (and etc.) morality should become *men's* morality. This is a pragmatic age, and people want their 'good principles' to have relevance to their daily activities. An example of what I mean is the very successful Episcopal Church in Rye, New York, where the Rev. Mr. Phillips ties his sermons in with business ethics, political ethics, happenings and personalities in current events."

Besides current event comments and the sermon, the minister, a representative of the community, has a good forum in the letters columns of newspapers.

The Friends Committee on National Legislation has made a study of newspaper letter writing and comes up with these suggestions (adapted from its pamphlet "How to Write a Letter to the Editor").

1. Type your letter if possible. It should be double space and neat.

2. Keep your letter to 250 words or less. The more concise the better.

3. Treat only one topic in the letter. Your selection should be timely and newsworthy.

4. Polish up particularly your first sentence. It should be short and enticing.

5. If the letter is to be critical, begin with a positive word of appreciation, agreement or praise. The letter should also end on a constructive note.

6. Avoid uncharitable language. Be frank, but friendly.

7. Provide the truth that may have been omitted or obscured from your viewpoint in the item carried in the paper.

8. Use personal experiences, if they fit in and are in good taste.

9. Appeal to principles shared by your readers, such as fair play, justice and mercy.

10. Sign your name and give your address. Many letter readers make a practice of throwing away unread letters that are not signed.

"Don't give up looking for your letter too soon," says the author of the leaflet, J. Stuart Innerst. "It may not appear for ten days or even longer. Don't be discouraged if your letter is not printed. Try again. If one letter in ten is accepted, you have reached an audience large enough to make your effort worth while." He says that readership surveys show that the letters are among the best-read features in a newspaper.

Then there's column writing.

It brings prestige, creative expression, and a chance to sincerely put your faith across to a massive audience, millions maybe, instead of a few hundred or a thousand or two on Sunday.

But landing a column with a major newspaper and/or a syndicate is one of the toughest jobs. It's much easier to publish a half-dozen books with a big-name publisher than to become a successful religious columnist. They are rare. The number of newspapers carrying religious columns appears to be decreasing, probably because more are handling religion now as a separate beat employing religion editors, and so concentrate on developing local features, instead of using syndicated material. Of eight religion columnists who elected to answer two companion questions on a questionnaire to determine the ratio of current papers using columns compared to the peak reached with the same columns, only two said that their peak was their current number of subscribing papers. The other six reported that the peak reached with their columns was in the past. All totaled,

213 newspapers used the columns prepared by the eight in the past, but only 106 newspapers use the same columns today. Another dozen religion columnists answered one or the other of the companion questions, some giving current subscribing papers as high as 300, but without a peak to compare the trend further.

But even with religion column writing apparently on the wane, especially the mass syndication of a column, you can still be a columnist.

The nation's religious columnists tell you how—at least how they got into the field of writing religion columns for newspapers.

"A sermon that appealed to a Chicago *Tribune* employee, member of my church," says the Rev. Dr. Harold Blake Walker, pastor of the First United Presbyterian Church, Evanston, Illinois, got him started as a religion columnist. "The sermon was cut and rewritten for newspaper use," says Dr. Walker, himself a former Associated Press newsman. "The resulting article received considerable comment and resulted in a regular Sunday magazine column." His column, an inspirational sermonette, "Living Faith," reaches fifteen newspapers daily and/or on Sunday.

The Rev. Dr. Roy L. Smith, retired, former editor of the Methodist *Christian Advocate* and still writing an International Bible Lesson column for newspapers, traces his first journalism back to the age of eleven when he "was the 'neighborhood correspondent' for the county-seat paper of our rural section of Kansas." He kept writing for one newspaper after another, through high school and college and seminary. He was known by editors, and had the rare credentials of being both a clergyman and a newspaperman. "Upon graduation," he says, "I entered the Methodist ministry, being assigned to three small churches just outside a very good county-seat town. Within three weeks I had an assignment with the local daily for some general reporting. A little later an organization was set up to publicize that section of Kansas in the 'eastern papers' and I was assigned to the St. Louis *Post Dispatch,* the Kansas City *Star,* the Topeka *Capital,* the Hutchinson *News,* and the Wichita *Beacon.* The Chicago *Tribune* accepted an occasional article. I kept my strings and sent them in once a month, and there were a good many months when the total of the checks amounted to more than the salary paid me by my church." One of his first regular features, lasting twenty-one years and reaching 150 papers, was "Sentence Sermons," with short messages like "Don't knock the church. It may have improved since you were there last." The idea began as Roy Smith's Post-Card Pulpit, to be sent to a proposed list of 5,000, but the newspaper that was to print it took it on as a regular feature of its own.

Good public relations with the press appear helpful in getting a column rolling. Religious leaders whose ability and interest are known to the press through some previous contact or recommendation, are often invited from time to time to write a column. Examples of men requested by editors to write columns are the Rev. Dr. Charles L. Evans, who writes a Sunday-school lesson column for the Norfolk *Journal and Guide;* the Rev. Dr. Benjamin E. Mays, who writes "My View" for the Pittsburgh *Courier;* Rabbi Robert I. Kahn, of Congregation Emanu El, Houston, Texas, who writes "Lessons for Life" for the Houston *Chronicle;* and the Rev. Dr. Herbert Spaugh, of the Little Church on the Lane, Charlotte, North Carolina, who writes "Everyday Counselor" for more than twenty papers reaching a circulation of around a million.

"My column commenced twenty-five years ago at the request of the Charlotte *News* which wanted a religio-psychological column to reach the man in the street," says Dr. Spaugh. "I did not commence the assignment until I had written twenty-five columns so that I would have a back-log after I commenced."

But successful columnists have begun by approaching editors on their own. A. F. Lokey, who writes "Bible Guidepost" for the Birmingham *News* and four other newspapers six days a week, says his column started twelve years ago. He was seventy at the time. "I showed the editor samples of my work. With my application, I presented an endorsement from a Dr. Edmunds, an outstanding preacher, scholar, and writer, who was listed in *Who's Who in America*."

Several report beginning a column as "a labor of love," then watching it grow in acceptance.

"I began in 1925 contributing a Daily Prayer free to the Spartansburg (South Carolina) *Herald*," says the Rev. Dr. John Marvin Rast, executive secretary, Methodist Board of Education, South Carolina Conference. He reaches six newspapers now, among them the Cincinnati *Enquirer* with his "Altar Stairs" or "Beginning the Day." The Daily Prayer column, he says, "continued for five years, then in the Sunday edition I began contributing a devotional meditation similar to the present releases. Then I began in January, 1934, contributing for remuneration my present daily feature, and added newspapers, then placed it with a syndicate." His column begins with a quotation from a noted person or the Bible, comments on it in a few lines and concludes with a few lines of Scripture and a prayer.

Another Methodist, William W. Reid, retired director of the Department of News Service, Methodist Board of Missions, New York City, says he started his "News in the World of Religion" in 1940 and "through church papers, I offered it to pastors to offer (free) to their local newspaper editors. The promotion has always been done by pastors showing samples to editors."

Columnists are specialists—whether on politics, science, religion or another subject. And they are usually specialists on an aspect of their specialty.

"Having written several histories of Catholic religious societies," says Glenn D. Kittler, who writes "The New Apostles," a series of profiles of missionaries, syndicated by the National Catholic Welfare Conference to fifteen newspapers, "I felt a column on mission personalities would be of interest and perhaps stir mission support. I suggested the column to the NCWC and it was accepted."

The Rev. Dr. Carlyle Adams, pastor of First Presbyterian Church of Rennsselaer, New York, drew upon a specialty to write a question and answer column, "Our Religions," for twenty-five newspapers, including the *Evening Star,* Washington, D.C., served by the *Register* and *Tribune* Syndicate. "The idea began when I was chaplain of Park College, Parkville, Missouri, in 1943," he says. "I used to have 'Question Hour' in the chapel. Students wrote questions. Then when I was doing a column for the Albany *Times-Union,* people began sending in questions." He draws on a large library of his own, a Franciscan Seminary and local rabbis to answer questions of all faiths.

A columnist, as do most serious free-lance writers, builds slowly, and scientifically. He does not shoot for the moon with the first product of his pen. "I began with a couple of articles for the Atlanta *Journal,*" says the Rev. John R. Brokhoff, who writes for the Charlotte *Observer.* "Later I wrote a daily column for two weeks for Charles Allen for the Atlanta *Constitution.* Then again I was guest columnist for Dr. Herbert Spaugh, Charlotte *News.* Finally, the *Observer.*"

The religion columnists generally keep "no daily schedule" and spend one to three hours a week for each column. One who writes a daily meditation says he spends one hour for each meditation and does them together—another, who writes a weekly column, says he "may work all morning on one, or polish it off in an hour and a half." Several such as Rabbi Kahn and the Rev. Webb B. Garrison, of Indianapolis, who prepare weekly columns, write a month's copy at one time each month.

Columnists have to be brief. How do clergymen, who are used to considerable latitude in preaching, limit their remarks to a tenth or a twentieth of the space they have, if they were writing a sermon? Their secret is, they say: "I just stop at end of one page; it requires a good deal of study to boil down the material or choose one specific aspect of a topic for writing within the word limits"; "talent . . ."; "count the words"; "a rigid scheme, 57 lines of not over 75 characters to the line";

"with dictaphone dictating machine, mark dictation slip to the proper length, and dictate to it"; "edit down to necessary length"; "edit and re-edit and sacrifice my best prose."

"Sometimes I write several articles on the same subject," says Mr. Lokey. "Thorough mastery of English is helpful." Benjamin Mays says, "I seldom run over. Practice helps to keep the article from being too long."

Religion columnists report extensive file systems, with as many as 30,000 items clipped as in the case of Dr. Walker. Glenn Kittler gets many of his leads from reading, he says, "but I also buy ideas from professional researchers." The Rev. B. H. Logan, who writes "The Church World" for the Pittsburgh *Courier,* reports "one file by topics, one by denominations, one for local, the other for publication." Columnists also admit to the addiction of being "constant carriers of notebooks." "Ideas are everywhere," says Fred Dodge, a trade association executive secretary who writes a "Minute Message" twice a week for fifteen newspapers, among them the Augusta (Georgia) *Herald.*

What is the biggest problem a clergyman has, if he aspires to be a newspaper columnist? Men who have made the grade as religion columnists call these their biggest stumbling blocks:

"To know how to write in newspaper style. Be brief. Short sentences. Write opposite from the way I preach. The important thing should be said in the first sentence" (Dr. Spaugh).

"Being accepted" (Rabbi Kahn).

"Overcoming the denominational label" (Dr. Smith).

"To get fresh material that will appeal to a wide readership" (Mr. Garrison).

"To get out of the pulpit; determine to meet deadlines. Too many clergymen can't forget they are always right" (Mr. Dodge).

"To learn to write with a readable style" (Dr. Walker).

"To overcome lack of experience in writing" (Rev. William E. Gilroy, retired NEA columnist).

"To keep a balance of news—not to overdo material for my own church" (Mr. Reid).

"Learning to be concise and practical" (Carl Yoder, who writes church-page short features for twenty-five papers).

"The big problem is to find time for concentrated, unhurried writing for meditation and research," according to the Rev. Dr. Adiel J. Moncrief, who has been writing an "Inspiration" column for the St. Joseph (Missouri) *Union-Observer,* and who after fifteen years as a pastor in St. Joseph is now church editor of the *Tribune-Times,* Tampa, Florida. With Dr. Moncrief, Columnists Brokhoff, Rast, Evans agree.

A National Council of Churches syndicated writer reports that the clergyman's biggest problem is "conciseness, ability to use layman's language, and a tendency to 'piosity.' Which is greatest depends on the man."

To what extent pulpit experience is helpful to the religious columnist depends on whom you ask. Most believe preaching helps, "Because in the pulpit one has a living visible audience and it is important for a columnist not to lose the common touch." Others say, "It is of no value" or, "It neither helps nor hinders." Another says, "I think preaching would hinder objective reporting; but that would depend on whether the column was news or opinion."

Says veteran preacher-writer Roy Smith: "The preaching style and the writing style are two entirely different matters. I *never* dictate anything I am going to submit for publication, for the moment I begin talking I find myself in a pulpit, and the reading effect is an entirely different matter. I make a very serious effort to keep the two styles distinct and different."

Religion columnists who must communicate to people of all faiths have to learn how to handle delicate controversial subjects: "Never comment on the controversy in my own name," is the way W. W. Reid stays out of the kettle on a hot issue. "Try to give balanced quotations on both sides from others." "I tell the truth as I see it," says Glenn Kittler. "I give the facts as I see them with sympathy and understanding," says Benjamin Mays. "My main purpose is to help people to find Christ and then to grow in grace and in knowledge, and controversial material is not needed," says A. F. Lokey. "Incorporate the contro-

versial material in a human-interest anecdote," says Webb
Garrison.

The columnists suggest, in the way of principles to guide the
prospective columnist, "Always ask, What will that fellow on
the assembly line think of this?"; "Use short, simple sentences
and simple language"; "Feel the color and drama of it"; "Make
it simple so the most unlearned can understand"; "Write only
what would challenge and interest you if you were the reader";
"Study the technique of newspaper and magazine feature writers"; "Make but one point in the article"; "Bring in incidents
and illustrations where possible"; "Find the one right short
illustration or picture"; "Use action verbs, make pictures with
words and accuse, condemn and execute every cliché"; "Write
in newspaper style—keep a little humor wherever possible";
"First sentence must attract attention—second sentence must
arouse curiosity—after that the rest is easy"; "Write with imagination"; "Present one idea, illustrate it, and drive the point
home"; "No preaching, no argument, quote others where opinion is involved."

"My advice to ministers who want to write religious columns
is purely mechanical," says D. K. Woodman, the Mansfield
(Ohio) *News-Journal* editor who syndicates forty-part Lenten
episodes called "Memo to Caesar." "Write six, submit them to
your local editor or to a syndicate, and remember that to get
published your stuff has to be more interesting than anything
else the newspaper could put in that space."

Now just what are you going to write about, if you aspire to
be a columnist?

"In a local community, any pastor should be able to furnish
a column of comment on the passing scene," says W. W. Reid.
"Christian principles could be applied to anything going on in
the community and in the world."

The columnists were asked to give some suggestion for a
"new religious column that you think could be written in daily
or weekly newspapers by a clergyman, if he is equipped in
ambition and ability for the task."

Among suggestions were: "Relate religion and health; people

are hungry for this"; "comparative religions"; "perhaps one dealing directly with controversial subjects, not taking sides but making the issues clear, and the alternatives"; "a *very* 'down to earth' column dealing with the application of Judeo-Christian ethics to contemporary issues in the news"; "the church around the world"; "brief biographies of the saints of all ages" (this, however, is being done for General Features Corporation very ably by Dr. Howard Harper, an Episcopalian, who each week features an event or saint from church history which is being commemorated, in the following week, as though it has just happened); "relevant religion"; "interpretation of the Christian cause as a world panacea for secularism and paganism"; "I have long thought that a two-inch single-column feature to be entitled 'Two Inches of Inspiration' might click."

But don't take these suggestions for new columns very seriously. The idea should be yours. "If the clergyman is 'equipped in ambition and ability,'" says Kittler, "he will think up his own ideas." It is hard to ride on someone else's ideas. How marketable an idea suggested by someone else would be for you is questionable. "If I had it I'd market it myself," says Dodge.

This author has come up with an idea for a column as a result of querying the men above, but he isn't going to tell. He can only say, nobody else is doing it and there seems to be a good need for it. He's first going to polish off four or five choice samples, launch them in one medium—either the newspaper for which he works or elsewhere—free lance (if someone else thinks the idea is marketable), then take clips and try to interest a syndicate or other papers individually. You can act similarly with your own idea. Try to free lance it first to one medium. You wouldn't know where to begin with my idea and you would have no real heart for it. You have to start your own idea-mill grinding, which puts us back to the main point of this chapter, that newspapering begins with sharpening the sense of creativity. You have to be involved with life, and have a reservoir for not only anecdotes and illustrations but a milieu which finds you responding, reacting to stimuli created by other persons and the issues which the human community are involved in today. You've got to be on your feet, to stand and to run, before you can type. The best newspaper copy is derived, not contrived.

Doing, not conceptualizing or spinning priceless rhetoric, is the way to acquiring newspaper space.

"Not every one that saith unto me, Lord, Lord, shall enter into the kingdom of heaven," said Jesus. He could have added, ". . . nor should he enter into print." "But he that doeth the will of my Father which is in heaven." The concrete acts of mercy are more likely to make print than the hard, correct repetition of the traditional creed or the mouthing of indisputable generalizations about the enemies of our times. "Whosoever heareth these sayings of mine, and *doeth* them, I will liken him unto a wise man, which built his house upon a rock: And the rain descended, and the floods came, and the winds blew, and beat upon that house; and it fell not: for it was founded upon a rock."

2

Free-Lance Writing:
Your Golden Opportunity

WEBB B. GARRISON

WRITING AS A "free lance," strictly on your own, offers you more rewards than any other avocation or hobby you can adopt.

In your basic role of prophet/preacher, you are deeply involved in communication. Most of it is oral and face-to-face. Yet it has many features in common with written communication directed to readers not likely to be met in person. In writing as in preaching, a sense of message—something to say—is basic. Both writing and speaking rest upon the same foundation of skills. So it is logical for you to put together articles or books made up of written words, as well as sermons composed of spoken ones.

SOME REWARDS FROM WRITING

No message is transmitted unless there is at least one receiver, whose function is as vital as that of the sender. Because that is the case, every person who feels he has a message is eager to get as many receivers as possible.

A larger audience is the first, and perhaps the most important, reward to be gained through writing. There are conspicuous individual exceptions; but in general, written material reaches more persons than do spoken messages.

In spite of such news media as radio and television, the average minister's chances of multiplying his audience center in the printed word. Weekly newspapers, barely able to survive, claim more constituents than most big churches. Sunday school publications and minor national magazines often reach as many as 100,000 persons. Even when circulated in only a few thousand copies, books are likely to influence large numbers of readers over a period of years or generations.

Soren Kierkegaard had only a small following during his life. But he knew written words usually outlive spoken ones. So he described a book as a traveler, setting out to trudge the highways until meeting the reader for whom it is meant: "that individual whom it seeks, toward whom, as it were, it stretches out its arms; that individual who is benevolent enough to let himself be found, benevolent enough to receive it."*

How few or how many such "benevolent" ones are met by a message, its author may never know. Whether actual or potential, the larger audience offered by the written word, as compared with that spoken from the pulpit, vastly enhances the messenger's sense of reward.

Feed-back effects upon preaching add to the writer's satisfaction. For the process of preparing a message for possible publication involves sharpening one's skills as a communicator.

You cannot—simply cannot—write words in any significant quantity without fostering consciousness of vocabulary, style, sentence and paragraph structure, and a host of related factors. Facility gained in writing will have great influence upon your speaking. If you devote even a few hours a week to putting words upon paper, you will gain insights and skills that will affect the way you utter words from the pulpit.

"My tongue is the pen of a ready writer," exulted David (Psalm 45:1). Training and exercise and study tend to enhance one's ability to handle the mechanics of communication. Sheer hard work will enable most persons to develop a style that is fluent and individual as well as "correct." So every hour devoted to writing is actually a self-taught laboratory in speaking.

Pleasure of creativity, say many ministers who write, makes the discipline worth while even if no manuscript ever wins an editor's approval. In its most sublime forms, delight is linked with fruitfulness. To create, to originate, to beget is to share in

---

* *Edifying Discourses,* Paul L. Homer, ed. (Harper Torchbooks, 1958), p. 1.

the on-going work of the Creator who wove this divine capacity into the creature, man.

A sermon or an article, a devotional talk or an essay, constitutes an offspring of your mind and soul. Like that preaching which yields its own reward through the shaping and making public of a message, writing at its best is joyful. Wholehearted praise of God needs no justification in terms of tangible "results."

No matter how ardently one strives, he will never be able to say he has heard all God's messages or accepted all God's bounties. So the pursuit of ways to make public those good gifts that one has himself accepted, is the most thrilling of all adventures. To witness, whether orally or in writing, is to engage in a quest that makes big game hunting seem dull. One who pursues this path to adventure will never become bored.

Income from writing is therefore the least important of its varied rewards. A minister who writes for the sake of his literary earnings is likely to trip over his checks. Payment must always be incidental, a by-product if it is not to become a stumbling block.

With this warning underscored, let's face it: except for small newspapers and a very few magazines of low circulation, publishers make it a standard practice to pay for material they use. Rates vary from a few dollars per thousand words, to extremely generous payment. Most standard book publishers offer royalty contracts to authors. Ten per cent of the retail price of copies sold is the most frequent royalty basis in the United States.

DEMANDS OF WRITING

It would be false to stress the rewards of writing without recognizing that there are also demands. One does not gain the prize without straining his legs and lungs in competition.

Hard work and self-discipline is the most obvious cost of elevating free-lance writing into an avocation. One simply does not produce a manuscript without putting words together in sequence, upon paper! For every minister who actually submits his material to editors, there must be at least two dozen, equally talented, who stop at the stage of wishful thinking.

One-of-these-days and When-I-have-an-easier-year are not familiar names on dust jackets. Writing (like preaching) is work . . . hard work. Only that person willing to pay the price of devoting hours and energy to pen or typewriter, has the slightest chance of seeing the progeny of his mind and spirit assume form as printed messages.

Unfailing optimism is as essential as hard work. For the nature of communication is such that there is some degree of "misunderstanding" as well as of understanding every time one makes public a message—whether it be written or oral. Preaching has pitfalls enough; one must pour out his heart, often without measurable results, yet somehow find for next Sunday both a new message and the courage to offer it.

Free-lance writing is even less predictable, because an editor's requirements of the moment may determine whether or not he accepts a given manuscript. That is, a written message that would get quick acceptance one week may be rejected the next. Variables are more complex and numerous than those which make preaching so demanding and challenging.

That person who is incurably hopeful, who refuses to take any "no" as final, has leaped across one of the biggest hurdles in the writer's life. Some specific practices for persistent and hopeful submission of manuscripts are discussed below, in the section on placement of material.

Other recreations must take second place. Golf, fishing, and television mix poorly with writing. So do lodge activities and civic clubbing. For as diverse as these interests are, each is like every other in that it requires time and interest.

In order to write in any appreciable volume, some other activities must be given up. It is as simple—and as complex—as that. Unless you are willing to schedule a weekly block of time for writing, you'll never make a start. Once you do, though, chances are good that you'll join hundreds of other ministers in concluding that rewards of writing greatly outweigh costs.

KINDS OF NONFICTION

A few ministers and ex-ministers have become famous for their short stories and novels. Large numbers of others have found their greatest satisfaction in writing nonfiction, which is much more closely related to their parish work. For this reason, as well as the fact that editors are now using clean, wholesome fiction in relatively small quantities, chances are good that you'll get special satisfaction from writing nonfiction.

Feature Article Versus Sermon

Regardless of its form, an article or feature is different from a sermon.

Exhortation plays an important role in preaching. There is a direct appeal to the heart as well as the head of the listener. It is not unusual to state a case, then devote much of the sermon to persuading listeners to accept a conclusion or act upon a challenge.

Articles have an entirely different focus. Though the writer may hope to persuade readers to adopt his point of view, direct appeals have little place in today's nonfiction. Using all the skill he has, the writer presents his case—then leaves it to readers to form their own conclusions.

This matter is so significant that it warrants illustration.

So many persons are wailing about the shortcomings of modern youth that a declaration of faith in youth should win a hearing. But treatment will vary widely, depending upon whether a sermon or a magazine article is the vehicle for the message.

Samuel's boyhood could be a foundation for a sermon. Contrast between piety of the youth and degeneration of highly respected elders might be stressed. Then listeners could be urged to have faith in today's boys and girls, challenged to think twice before regarding all adolescents as potential delinquents.

As I handled this theme for *American Family* magazine,

there was no Scripture reference. (Few secular magazines publish articles that include Biblical quotations.) An incident from the boyhood of Augustine formed a 500-word introduction. Then the career of the theologian was traced from turbulent student days to his triumphant death. Two closing paragraphs pointed out that no boyhood acquaintance of Augustine could have predicted his influence upon Christendom. Published under the title, "This Younger Generation," the article left it for readers to draw parallels between the trouble-maker of Tagaste and hot-rodders of their own communities.

Preachers tend to spell out their conclusions, then urge that they be adopted. Magazine writers set up situations in which their conclusions are as logical as possible, then hope their readers will take the last step or two by themselves.

Sometimes a pulpit message has little factual material in it; exhortation is the mood. That is why "sermonizing" has become a derogatory term in some quarters. Specific facts—names, places, dates, and the like—may make up the bulk of a feature article. One of the big problems confronting a veteran preacher who wishes to begin writing for magazines, is his tendency to employ sermonic style.

To sharpen your consciousness of differences in the two approaches, make a paragraph-by-paragraph analysis of samples. Dissect a sermon in your favorite preachers' magazine, then compare it with an article in *Reader's Digest*. In a recent sermon of your own, count the sentences that communicate no information. Then compare the percentage of such material with "exhortation" in a popular magazine article.

Your findings will help you to recognize other distinctions, such as those between a feature article and a personal essay. Four types of magazine nonfiction offer special opportunities to ministers; perhaps you will wish to try your hand at each of them.

Research Articles

As its name implies, a research article is written by finding specific information to form a vehicle transporting the idea you wish to make public. Perhaps you have at first nothing but a pet peeve—or a zeal for reform. Having stood at the altar to baptize a boy with a name no baby should have thrust upon him, you'd like parents to think twice.

That's the beginning of a feature article.

But you need facts—not impressions or judgments of your own. For this or any other subject to be treated in feature style, there are several standard sources of material: books and magazines, interviews, and specialized publications. To investigate each of these areas may require considerable time; my own article on how *not* to name the baby appeared in *Your Life* many months after the idea was conceived.

First, I made a folder and labeled it "names of children." Everything that I happened to discover that bore on the subject went into that folder. Over a period of weeks, it came to include a dozen newspaper clippings. There were also scribbled notes from casual reading and conversation with friends. While in no sense formal, this is genuine research. Often it makes a major contribution to a nontechnical manuscript.

Second, I consulted the local library. Indexes to periodicals listed several articles that had some connection with naming children. It's unusual if all the articles listed in such guides prove to be available locally, but there are few counties without a library that includes at least a basic collection of bound periodicals.

Importance of library research is a variable, depending both upon the subject you are treating and the magazine for which you expect to write. If you hope to appear in *Religion in Life,* you will have to be somewhat academic and "scholarly" in your approach. But if (like me) you are more interested in *Christian Herald,* it will be necessary to keep the bones of your library work from showing above the surface of your article.

Personal interviews and letters constituted the third area of research for my exhortation to new parents. I knew that Almerindo Portfolio had been treasurer of New York under LaGuardia, so I wrote asking how he got that name. Judge Kennesaw Mountain Landis was famous in the baseball world; it was logical to inquire whether he was born at the time of the Civil War battle. (He was—and rejoiced that he did not make his advent at the time of the Battle of Bull Run!)

Several persons in my community had names that seemed a bit queer. I conducted an informal poll, asked them how they got their names and whether they liked them. Surprisingly many persons confessed they'll never forgive their parents for their names. But a woman named Mary may be no happier with her lot than a neighbor whose birth certificate reads "Bo Peep."

Don't fall into the error of thinking you can't write research articles unless you have access to a major library. Just as you can interview by mail, so you can get much published material simply by asking. Public relations departments of major corporations will cheerfully send leaflets and booklets related to their special interests. Life insurance companies offer an amazing array of top-quality literature on a variety of subjects; most of it is free.

Many technical books on the Bible and religion may be borrowed by mail. Consult a nearby university of your denomination, or see the discussion in *The Preacher and His Audience* (Fleming H. Revell Co., 1954), pages 144ff. Visit the library of your nearest tax-supported college and ask what privileges are available to you. Get acquainted with representatives of federal and state governmental agencies whose interests bear upon subjects on which you'd like to write. From leaflets to thick books, free and low-cost material in great variety may be secured from the U. S. Government Printing Office, Washington.

Personal Essays

Sometimes called a "think piece," a personal essay is a narrative of opinion or experience. First-person style is often used. A vivid experience, personal problem, victory over a difficulty, pet peeve or program of reform may be the source of an essay. Religious, ethical, and moral subjects lend themselves to effective treatment in this style.

An essay may be designed to provide explanation, persuade readers to action, or simply to entertain. It may be largely a "confession" on the part of the author, or may rest upon views and experiences of others.

Seasonal themes lend themselves to essay style, so religiously-oriented subjects treated in this fashion often appear in secular magazines at Christmas, Easter, Mother's Day, and Thanksgiving. Since readers have established interest in such seasonal pieces, a familiar emphasis treated in slightly different style has a good chance of winning editorial approval.

An essay of my own gave a bit of a twist to the Thanksgiving theme by suggesting that "It Pays To Be Thankful!" As published in *Journal of Living,* the piece rested largely upon everyday experiences in which conscious gratitude yielded dividends. A few biographical anecdotes of the type commonly used for sermon illustrations provided human interest, helped persuade readers that the author's case was not unique.

Most editors not only accept humorous essays; they scramble eagerly for good ones! It is far harder to achieve the light touch of, say, Jean Kerr, than it would seem from hastily reading a collection of her pieces. But you'll find it fun to try your hand mocking some practice or idea to which you object, as a way of asking readers to accept your view. Even if humor proves not quite your field, you'll enjoy experimenting to find out how words are compounded to produce laughter. Should you discover that the humorous essay come easily for you, editors will rejoice when you have a manuscript for them.

One of the few satirical pieces that I've written grew out of a personal annoyance. A persistent door-to-door salesman made such a nuisance of himself that I decided to strike back by spoofing him and his tribe. Entitled "How to Say 'No' to a Salesman," the piece rested upon a twelve-point sales formula used to instruct peddlers.

Each bit of advice for the salesman was inverted—turned inside out, as it were—and applied to intended victims. Salesmen are urged to keep conversation under control and hold attention of prospects; I suggested that the sales-resister prepare conversational gambits in advance and be fortified with pictures of the grandchildren to hold attention of the salesman.

That topic has no direct connection with the minister's major concerns. But spokesmen for religion overlook a powerful tool for shaping opinion when they fail to make deliberate use of humor. A barrage of laughter may have greater impact than a frontal attack upon some bastion of the Evil One.

Whether humorous or serious, personal essays require much less time than articles based upon research. Their relatively close affinity with sermons is an added reason for making some experiments in this medium a "must" for the minister/writer.

Short Features

Most national and regional magazines include brief nonfiction. Length may vary from a single sentence to 500 words. Epigrams, anecdotes, jokes, personal experiences, and factual oddities are in constant demand. A few major magazines even purchase quotations selected by free-lance contributors.

Among professional writers, such items are often termed "filler material." That name came into vogue when editors actually selected brief pieces in order to fill small areas of white space at the ends of columns. Readers have demonstrated such great interest in short features that they are now important in their own right. It is not unusual for an editor deliberately to cut material from a story or article in order to break the monotony of type by inserting a "filler."

Such material offers the beginning writer a particularly good field. For one thing, individual filler items are used in greater number than any other type of nonfiction. Consequently, chances of acceptance are multiplied.

Again, your investment of time and work is comparatively small. A dozen or more short features may be prepared in half the time required for one 2500-word article based on research.

Finally, the professional writer who has mastered the craft and begun to build a reputation, is likely to concentrate upon longer pieces. When you are trying to win approval for brief features, the level of competition isn't quite so high as in the case of full-length format.

Many kinds of material can be handled in brief format. Dr. Wallace Fridy, of Columbia, S. C., has built a wide readership for short prayers published in a string of daily newspapers. Meditations and devotional pieces, often kept under 100 words, are used in many periodicals with general readership. Epigrams are favored by some of the nation's top magazine editors. Anecdotes of the type found in books of sermon illustrations are frequently used as fillers, but require careful rewriting and slanting to the readership of the magazine at which they are aimed.

Short features of top quality require long work! Specialized ones such as those which appear in *Reader's Digest* and *Saturday Evening Post* often demand as much work as a full-length feature article designed for a magazine of low circulation.

In spite of obstacles at the top of the magazine world, the door is wide open at lower levels. Any minister willing to work faithfully at preparation of short features has a good chance of breaking into print through this avenue. In the process of doing that, he enhances his skill in the use of words and placement of manuscripts, so prepares himself for undertaking more difficult projects.

Material for Religious Magazines

On the surface, it would seem that Sunday-school periodicals of your denomination would offer the ideal outlet for your literary activity. But the opposite is the case. General secular magazines are far more likely to use your work than are lesson publications of the church.

Part of this paradox is due to radical differences in ways the two sets of editors secure their material. Much of the contents of any general magazine is likely to be made up of articles and features selected from unsolicited contributions. Per cent of staff-written and assigned material varies from one periodical to another, of course. But few major secular magazines are absolutely closed to the free lance; some depend entirely upon unsolicited manuscripts.

Sunday-school quarterlies and monthlies, on the other hand, are written almost entirely upon assignment. Topics and methods of treating lessons are selected many months in advance. Then editors approach writers already known to have competence, and arrive at contracts or agreements by which manuscripts are prepared to specification.

Until you have published elsewhere, it is all but useless to offer your services as a lesson writer. Once you have a few samples of published material, it is appropriate to ask that you be considered for Sunday-school lesson work. However, schedules in this field are such that it may take a year or two to get an invitation, even if your published work pleases editors of a lesson periodical.

That isn't the case with story papers and general religious magazines. Like the secular press, these media depend heavily upon free-lance writers. So do many Catholic periodicals. Since the Roman Catholic Church does not issue Sunday-school quarterlies, their place is taken by an imposing list of high-quality general magazines.

Obviously, you wouldn't wish to write upon subjects that require treatment you can't use in integrity. But many non-ecclesiastical subjects are free of such problems, and Catholic editors are not so much interested in a writer's background as in what he has to say. At *Catholic Home Messenger,* for example, editors told me they do not know the faith of one contributor in ten. Because national Catholic magazines greatly outnumber Protestant ones, and because they have established interest in subjects with which ministers naturally deal, opportunities in this field are inviting.

Books

Partly as an effect of television's early years and partly as a result of other influences, book reading (and therefore, publishing) went through a period of relative listlessness in the last two decades. Now that the newness has begun to wear off television, large numbers of persons are turning back to books. This trend is accelerated by both the growth in population and the increasing emphasis upon higher education.

So the United States book publishing field is booming.

Much of the spectacular gain is in specialized fields: textbooks, paperback editions, and children's books. But along with these segments of the book publishing industry, the general or "trade" lists are also showing healthy gains both in number of titles issued and level of sales.

As you contemplate the rewards and challenges in the book field, always remember that many factors are controlled by the economics of publishing. Rising costs of production mean that a publisher will lose money unless he succeeds in selling several thousand copies of a volume.

What are the implications for you?

One factor is especially important. Unless your manuscript is directed to a reasonably large audience, its very nature reduces the likelihood of publication. Again, rising costs mean that publishers can seldom take a chance on a book that they judge strong enough to attract only local buyers.

Because a book must have inner unity, it must be more than

simply a collection of articles or sermons. Aside from this factor, sermons offer you less opportunity than any other kinds of material. That's partly because publishers are constantly deluged with manuscripts from ministers who have put a dozen or so of their best sermons into writing. But an equally important factor is that, except in rare cases, books of sermons are bought only by ministers—who seldom buy enough copies of a given book to let the publisher recover his investment.

Make a careful study of existing books that are closely related to a book you'd like to write. Try to find out what ingredients in these books gave them a "plus" quality. Analyze the lists of publishers in whom you are interested, in order to discover what kinds of books they usually issue. Then produce a manuscript aimed at a specific group of readers for whom one or more firms publish regularly.

In many instances, you'll save time and postage by sending a letter of inquiry rather than submitting an entire book manuscript "cold." A brief outline—with a few sample pages—will give editors some indication of both your subject and the skill with which you handle words. As a rule, though, any editor who shows interest will want to see a completed manuscript and not simply a chapter or two. These factors add up to a rule of thumb procedure: analyze your potential readership and potential publisher before starting to write; produce a completed manuscript; submit an outline or synopsis until you find an editor willing to take a look at the entire manuscript.

SOURCES AND DEVELOPMENT OF IDEAS

Your experience in writing sermons and talks gives you a natural advantage at this point. For articles, short features, and books are born in about the same fashion as sermons. Style of development is different, but each case requires that difficult first step: selecting something that forms a suitable subject for treatment.

Interest is the first requirement. Unless you are interested in a topic, you'll find it difficult to interest others. But if you are so absorbed with an idea that you are possessed by it, there's a chance that you may develop it in such fashion that others will follow your lead. As a working rule, anything that has genuine interest for you is a potential subject for a book, article, or short feature.

Probably you already have an established routine for saving sermon ideas. If so, you can use the same pattern or a modification of it in your free-lance writing. Whether for oral or written development, the majority of ideas seem to come from a few reasonably well-defined areas of life.

Problems Have Power

Everybody has problems; everybody is eager for solutions, and grateful to anyone who can offer valid ones. So the printing press is as natural a medium as the pulpit for offering ways men may meet their problems.

In order to write about a problem, it is necessary to recognize that it exists! That may sound strange, but until I began working with a few parolees in a down-town church, I did not dream the extent of their special problem: getting that first job after release from prison. Most employers will take a chance on an ex-prisoner who has done satisfactory work for a period. Few employers are willing to give such a man that essential first chance.

Here is a problem with potential for emotion-packed treatment. But the number of parolees is relatively small. They do not form a substantial segment of the magazine audience. In order to win a place in a magazine of wide circulation, the problem must be important to many readers. Rehabilitation of criminals has significance for everyone. Treated as the crucial step in rehabilitation, the matter of providing that first job for a parolee assumes general interest and is suitable for any of two dozen major magazines. Therefore that idea from immediate pastoral experience will go into my own "futures" list.

Your everyday work throws you into intimate personal contact with a great variety of persons. More than any other man in the community, you come into first-hand contact with human problems, burdens, and victories. You are constantly bombarded with opportunities to see dilemmas for which faith offers a solution. Every time you see such a problem and develop a workable solution that can be used by a substantial number of persons, you have an idea for a manuscript of wide appeal.

Confession is Contagious

Evangelists know that nothing exceeds the power of a religious testimony by a person vividly aware of divine aid. "It happened to me" gives power and authenticity to what one says.

In the same way, actual participation by a writer tends to make his reports interesting and convincing. Almost any vivid experience can be the seed of an idea for a magazine article.

Once I engaged in a heated debate with a group of friends. Some insisted that dignity is the first essential in religious music. Others argued that rhythm and melody should be popular in style. As an outgrowth of that discussion, I visited my first "all night gospel singing." Notes made during two and one-half hours of gospel music formed the basis of a first-person report published in *The Christian Advocate*.

Since your own experience is necessarily limited, you can extend it by interviews. If you know a person whose religious service has been filled with color and adventure, interviews with him or her will provide material that has all the impact of a personal confession.

Perhaps my own most unusual idea of this sort came from reading a three-line news item. According to it, a chaplain was spending the Antarctic night with men at the South Pole. In this instance, my correspondence was literally global! Information gathered through questions asked at a distance of 9,000 miles gave vividness to a report that showed religious service isn't limited to the comfortable and conventional.

Special Interests Tug and Pull

Nearly every special category of reader is the basis for a magazine appealing to narrow interests. It's hard to think of a subject-matter specialization, or a segment of the population, for whom no periodical is published.

In your daily activities, you see newspaper stories and hear comments about topics that interest you—and for which there are established groups of readers served by a special magazine. In such cases, there is no need to work to arouse interest; it already exists, and you have only to respond to that interest to win an acceptance.

After I had been free-lancing for a few years, my eye was caught by a report that Bobby Gordon, eleven, was given special permission to study chemistry at Western Reserve University. Such an item offered at least two possibilities for appealing to special interests of readers.

It could be developed as an article for chemistry teachers. But that readership is a small base for an article. Why not write for Bobby's contemporaries? Slanted to grade-school students, the article based on a boy's passion for chemistry appeared in *Open Road* under the title, "For Success Tomorrow, Harness Your Enthusiasm Now!"

Even when your attention is caught by an idea with nearly universal appeal, always think in terms of specific groups of readers and particular magazines. No matter how vivid an idea may be, it must be developed for a given audience—or readership. This factor is so crucial that it is treated at some length below, in the section on placement of material.

A Notebook is Essential

Every time you find an idea for an article or feature or book, *write it down*. Don't wait. Make a memo on the spot, if possible. It may be months or even years before you do anything about a particular bit of insight; no matter—*write it down!* As you go through your notebook (or filing system) from time to time discarding items that no longer command your interest, you may throw away 90 per cent of your ideas. Nevertheless, any time you have what at the moment seems a good idea, *write it down*.

Unless you take this matter seriously, and work at it faithfully, you will quickly exhaust your store of ideas and find that you have time and energy—but no channels through which they may flow to shape manuscripts. If you do cultivate the habit of saving every idea, at least until you have taken a second or third look at it, your list of future projects will grow longer every year. In time, you'll find that you have two or five or ten times as many ideas as you can translate into finished projects. Then, and only then, you can be highly selective in the choice of books and articles and features you actually complete.

It isn't enough, though, simply to jot down a memo: "heroism by ordinary folk." Analyze the subject and make it as precise as possible. Then note some of the groups of readers to whom that subject might appeal. It's fairly routine to talk about courage on the part of strong young men; why not concentrate upon elderly heroes and heroines?

Restricted in that fashion and deliberately slanted toward readers who seek courage through religion, "Heroism Knows No Age Limit" became a lead article in *Faith Today*. Nearly all the case histories used in that piece were furnished, by the way, in response to one inquiry directed to the Carnegie Hero Fund Commission.

Your notebook entries will be as valuable as you make them. For until an idea takes reasonably precise form *in relation to a specific audience*, it is all but worthless. "Faith" is too broad a subject for treatment in article form. "Faith's influence upon effects of surgery" might, just might, be a suitable subject. In order to stand a chance of publication in a magazine like *Today's Health*, meticulous research would be necessary. Half a dozen vivid case histories might form the basis for a piece slanted toward *Presbyterian Life*.

Chances of acceptance would be best if the piece could be

directed to readers among whom surgery is most common. Should *Journal of Lifetime Living* be your target, then it would be poor judgment to tell about faith of college students. Case histories should come from persons who have much in common with those who will read them—i.e., aging men and women, most of them retired.

Once you've developed the habit of keeping a notebook of specific themes and subjects plus potential groups of readers, you'll find that there is cross-fertilization between your preaching and your writing. Some of your sermons can be adapted to form superb feature articles, while some of your feature articles will contribute vivid illustrations and even complete subjects for your witnessing from the pulpit.

PRODUCING THE MANUSCRIPT

Always bear in mind that you cannot write for humanity in the abstract. Every manuscript you produce should be directed to a definite group of readers, whose interests and distinctive traits you bear in mind as you write. A discussion of free-lance writing as an avocation for public school teachers would have much in common with this chapter—but illustrative examples and emphases would have to be quite different. This aspect of writing becomes increasingly clear as experience is gained; in time, slanting toward a selected readership becomes automatic.

Neither this nor other skills can be cultivated purely by theoretical analysis. By far the best way to learn to write is . . . to write. Rules for paragraph structure, the introduction, and such matters, "come to life" only when considered against the background of actual manuscripts.

Make it a practice, therefore, to adhere to a definite production schedule: a particular number of pages written each week. From time to time, work through a textbook on writing nonfiction. Each time such a book is read, in the light of growing experience, it will prove more helpful.

There will be weeks when you have no free time. If you

mean business about writing, you must hold such barren periods to a minimum. Frequently you will have time, but lack inclination actually to put words on paper. Especially at first, it may be necessary to force yourself to make a start. Just as musicians get in the mood for a concert by tuning their instruments, so a writer can overcome a mental block by copying the last few paragraphs written the day before or turning to a feature in a current magazine and making an outline of its structure.

When possible, use comparatively big chunks of time for writing the first draft. Then put it aside for a few days; work of revising and copying can be done in briefer segments of time than those required for actual composition. Again, after even a brief interval you are likely to read your work more objectively than when it still glows from the heat of creativity. Revise material as many times as you think necessary, until it takes a form with which you are reasonably satisfied.

Do not wait for perfection, though. The worst that can happen is to get a series of rejections. Unless your work is put into the mail, you'll never know whether or not editors can use it. Work at continuous development of your own style, and growing skill in mechanics of writing. But give your best manuscripts a try even though you think you could improve them by another revision. If all your energy is concentrated upon writing, to the neglect of offering material for publication, you'll never break into print!

Vocabulary

Ministers are up to their necks in the sea of communication all the time, so surpass most persons in sensitivity to words. You already know that no communication takes place when you use words not in the vocabulary of your listeners. So you probably have developed a practice of avoiding long and technical terms.

At the same time, you face a danger peculiar to religious leaders. Some of the terms you use in your sermons may be anemic, even empty, because they are used so frequently and in so many senses. Cant phrases that get by in the pulpit show up glaringly in print. So you need to guard against the danger of leaning upon professional jargon.

Sentences and Paragraphs

Quite a bit has been said in recent years about "readability." Some analysts have gone so far as to devise formulas by which they claim to measure the ease or difficulty with which material can be read. While such findings are probably oversimplified and are challenged by the structure of many literary classics, readability is not to be ignored.

In general, it is well to strive for short words and direct sentences.

Most magazine editors also prefer manuscripts with comparatively brief paragraphs. Part of the reason lies in the physical makeup of the modern page. Since narrow columns are generally used, lengthy paragraphs form long blocks of unbroken type and appear formidable. Shorter paragraphs increase the amount of white space in a column, and probably do reduce the effort required in reading.

Many college professors tend to be patronizing or to sneer at mass circulation magazines whose editors stress ease of reading. That is not strange, for the classroom is a special and highly selective communication situation. Professors don't have to be lucid and entertaining; their listeners sit before them under duress.

Pay no attention, therefore, to academicians and literary dilettantes who look down their noses at any publication written and edited for millions of readers. For a really fruitful course in sentence and paragraph structure, spend a month in painstaking analysis of *Reader's Digest* articles.

Actually count the number of words in sentences, and the number of sentences in paragraphs. Revise printed sentences to change word order, and observe subtle effects upon meaning and impact. See how many noncommunicative words like "a" and "the" can be struck from a published article. Then go over your own most recent manuscript and see how much space is occupied by dead words.

Style

Literary style is as elusive as musical style. Though the eye of the listener can detect no difference between the way a bow is handled by the high-school music teacher and a budding Paganini, the two do not produce the same melodies. To say precisely how Shakespeare's style departs from that of a third-rate music hall hack, it would be necessary to be Shakespeare.

So all neat rules defining literary style are suspect.

Any person who writes in considerable volume over a long period, and who works at improving his way of putting words together, will develop his own style. Some qualities of a great writer can be "absorbed," as it were, by spending long hours analyzing his work. Jack London did that with the short stories of Rudyard Kipling, and became a self-taught master of that literary form.

Apart from such deliberate emulation of work that you admire, you will profit from comparing your own work with that of writers whom you like. Take an example of your best feature writing, and compare it with a *Pageant* article and a feature by Jim Bishop. Tear all three limb from limb to find both parallels and basic differences.

One thing you are likely to discover is that published copy employs vivid and specific words rather than general ones. Describing the hallway of a public school, an amateur might write about such items as "a bronze plaque flanked by an oil painting and portrait." Treated in professional style, the same ingredients might emerge as "The Gettysburg Address in bronze, flanked by a portrait of John Greenleaf Whittier and a 1937 oil painting entitled 'Harvest Time.'"

Work constantly at developing your skill in using words that point to things readers can see, touch, smell, taste, and hear. Avoid clichés and loose generalizations. Experiment with simple and compound sentences, direct and indirect sentence structure. Read samples of your copy aloud, so your ears will catch awkward bits leaped over by your eyes. Try to develop a mental image of the persons you hope will read a particular piece, and keep them in mind as you talk directly to them.

The Lead

With a clear mental image of readers in mind, you'll find it natural to select good material for your introduction, or "lead." As the latter term hints, a major function of the opening paragraph is to lead readers into the subject.

An effective lead must be directly related to the body of the article, and must have high interest value. Unless readers are attracted by the first few sentences, likelihood that they will finish an article is greatly reduced. Avoid, therefore, both the dull and the irrelevant.

Many writers and editors think a colorful anecdote is the best of all lead material. Vividness is not enough, though. It must also serve as a genuine introduction.

Odd bits of information of the "startling statement" type often make good leads. So do direct questions and summary statements. In the case of an essay, a graphic piece of description may be the most natural and compelling kind of introduction.

As with every other phase of writing, you'll profit from making an exhaustive study of introductions to articles that you like as a reader. Count the number of words used in introductions of published articles. Edit their lead paragraphs, to see how many words you can take out without weakening their impact. Make your own classification of kinds of introductions. Study old manuscripts to see whether you've tried all varieties of openings, or only one or two.

When you write an introduction to a new article, lay it aside for a day or two and then check it carefully.

Is it compact? Does it seem so condensed that it is crowded? Is there something here to catch a reader who isn't interested in the subject? Does the first paragraph include colorful words and phrases? names and happenings? conversation?

Is it easy to read, even aloud? Does it relate to some question that is currently in the news? Does it entice the reader to complete the article and find out what happens?

The Conclusion

Though the conclusion is not so difficult as the lead, it also has special traits that require careful writing. For an article that meanders or dribbles to a close is likely to leave readers vaguely dissatisfied.

That's why the first (and hardest) role of the conclusion is that of actually bringing a piece to a decisive, clear-cut close!

Speakers often find themselves at the end of a message, aware that they are through but vaguely dissatisfied. In such a situation, it's common to indulge in what psychologists call "talking past the point." Preachers who do it tend to go back over the whole argument of the sermon.

Just as a master comedian tells his jokes in such fashion that the punch line explodes suddenly and violently, so a literary craftsman builds power into his conclusion. He leaves the reader on a high level of interest, instead of continuing to labor his point so long that there is unconscious resistance: "He's already said that two or three times; why doesn't he quit?"

Written discourse has the advantage over spoken at this point, because practically all editors have fairly rigid length requirements. If *Guideposts* lists its needs as centering in 1200-word articles, you're wasting your time and postage to submit 3000-word manuscripts. Therefore, when you reach space limits established, you have no choice. You must bring your piece to a close.

In spite of this factor, a good conclusion usually leaves readers wanting more. This reaction is likely to hinge upon vividness in the final paragraph or two. Instead of driving the thesis home by means of exhortation, as in preaching, there must be something with real "content."

Conclusions fall into only a few categories: vivid anecdote, summary statement, challenge to action, and question that leaves a decision to the reader. In popular United States magazines, far more summary statements and anecdotes are used than any other kinds of conclusions.

As with leads, you'll learn more by painstaking study of samples—your own and those of other writers—than by reading about conclusions. Use this discussion, therefore, as a springboard from which to make a clean dive into the water and begin to swim!

CONFLICT IN NONFICTION

Everybody recognizes that novels and short stories require a pattern of conflict to hold interest of readers. Though the plot of a feature article is not always visible on the surface, it is as vital here as in the case of fiction.

If the reader knows how an article will end by the time he's finished the first few paragraphs, interest is likely to lag. So tension and struggle must be built into the development. A protagonist, or hero, must be challenged by some antagonist, or villain. Should it be obvious from the start that the hero will come out on top and how he'll do it, then conflict must revolve about his encounters with the villain.

"But that's absurd," you may retort. "There are lots of feature articles that deal with nonhuman factors and forces. In such cases, there's no one in the piece to play the role of hero."

It is precisely at this vital point that many beginning writers overlook a basic characteristic of nonfiction. When you depict struggle and build tension, a human protagonist isn't necessary. "Trust versus superstition" can be as thrilling as "detective versus gangster." For that reason, it is both appropriate and suggestive to speak of a feature article as a "story."

Deliberately think of your next manuscript as a *story* in order to sharpen consciousness of its plot. Be very clear in your own mind as to identity of protagonist and antagonist; make a list of ways these opponents clash, and the outcome of each encounter. Try to avoid letting the protagonist win too easy a victory; if he gets the worst of it in a couple of preliminary skirmishes, his ultimate triumph will be more vivid.

Perhaps a few case histories will help make some of these matters clear.

Novelty Versus Tradition

Though there are prominent exceptions, most Protestant clergymen select their field of service early. It is traditional in many denominations that a man should go through college and seminary, then serve a series of increasingly large congregations. It follows that the story of a man who departed from this pattern offers the conflict of novelty versus tradition.

So that's how I handled the biography of the Rev. Arthur E. Beckett. Pastor of First Methodist Church in Huntington, West Virginia, he earlier spent seven years in the same city. But his first term was not in religious service. Rather, he worked in pattern shops of the C&O Railroad. That background made him a natural subject for a profile in *Tracks* magazine, house organ of the C&O. In order to hold interest of porters and engineers, freight agents and roundhouse crews, a framework of struggle was essential. Beckett's departure from the conventional route into the ministry was a ready-made skeleton on which to hang such items as giving up a good job to enter college, and becoming pastor of men under whom he worked in his railroad years.

Initiative Versus Protection

Every mother and father face the problem of how much protection should be given to adolescents. Here is a pervasive point of tension in modern society. Therefore it should be a natural vehicle for developing a story on parental encouragement of initiative on the part of children.

As I handled this topic for *Woman's Life,* the first two paragraphs made it clear that I'd urge parents to confer responsibility and foster self-reliance in children. Yet the case against the overprotective parent wasn't painted entirely in black.

A two-paragraph summary of John Wesley's life showed that his emotional attachment to his mother spoiled him as a candidate for matrimony—and helped shape him for his role as reformer and church founder. Sharp contrast was provided by case histories from careers of George Westinghouse, Carl Linnaeus, and James McNeil Whistler—all of whom eventually rebelled against plans made for them by their parents.

Trust Versus Anxiety

Sermon themes often focus upon general problems that are suitable subjects for inspirational essays. That is clearly the case with the conflict between trust and anxiety. Here, the "plot" of an article is obvious. In order to develop a manuscript around it, the writer needs only to find suitable illustrative examples and organize them into a coherent argument.

Writing for *Challenge* magazine, I chose the title, "Are You Afraid of Mice?" Fear of mice was compared with anxiety about wars, depressions, and national disasters. In this instance, the antagonist of anxiety was challenged by making light of his threats as well as showing cases in which trust transformed life and gave strength to lift burdens.

Providence Versus Fate

Occasionally a writer will discover or stumble upon a basic plot that can be used, with only minor variations, for a multitude of themes. When that happens, he is in the position of a detective story writer whose successive stories employ new characters for the same old struggles.

Since I'm deeply interested in science and nature as well as in religion, it occurred to me some years ago that a God-centered interpretation of natural phenomena might interest readers. Several questions may be raised about any event or process whatever. Does it occur as a result of impersonal natural law, or is it the work of providence? What are man's assured findings, and what are his areas of ignorance? What dramatic incidents will illustrate the ceaseless struggle to overcome ignorance with truth?

Once this basic pattern of conflict became clear, I found that I could use it for a multitude of subjects. It is the skeleton on which I hung stories about phenomena as diverse as migration of birds, chemical composition of water, and influence of honeybees upon civilization. In the years since gaining some degree of competence in developing the case for divine care as opposed to blind natural law, I must have treated it at least fifty times. With style and subject matter adapted to the magazines for which particular manuscripts were prepared, this "plot" has been used for *Coronet, Natural History, Catholic Digest, Toronto Star Weekly, Science Digest,* and numerous lesser media.

You aren't likely to have the same enthusiasm I feel for this way of asking readers to vote for God. But there's a good chance that you have deeply established interests of your own about which a pattern of conflict can be built. Experiment until you find just the right vehicle in which to express your belief, then adapt the plot to a variety of specific subjects. When you do that, you will have found one of your own natural niches; here you can write easily, in considerable volume, with enormous satisfaction plus good chances of editorial acceptance.

TITLES FOR YOUR MANUSCRIPTS

Teachers of writing do not agree about the role and importance of titles. Some consider them of trifling significance, and point out that editors are often forced to discard good titles because of typographical factors. While that is the case, a surprisingly large number of editors will use titles as submitted, or modify them slightly.

Even if your title never gets into print, however, it has two major functions. Each is important in its own right. Together, these factors make it important that you work hard to get the best possible title for every manuscript you produce.

First, an editor must be attracted by a manuscript and "sold" on it before it has any chance to bid for a mass audience. In the case of small magazines, editors themselves often read every unsolicited contribution. Large magazines employ readers, whose job is to go through the daily quota of free-lance material and select pieces that deserve a second look.

Considerations of space and typography may automatically eliminate a good title from chances of being set at the head of an article. But that very title may be a factor in catching an editor's attention and persuading him that a manuscript is both interesting and professional in quality.

Again, the task of writing a title will help you sharpen your perspective and define your goals. No matter how cleverly worded, a title is of little value unless it suggests what is to be communicated. Make-up of the modern magazine automatically limits the length of titles. In effect, therefore, the writing of a title is an exercise in expressing ideas in half a dozen words or less.

Strong, colorful words are usually considered desirable in titles. To the degree that the title has "punch," it is likely to perform one of its major functions: catching the interest of readers.

Many editors do everything possible to pull readers into articles by working for "you appeal" in titles. As a casual reader, I'm likely to glance through a magazine and stop to read only those articles whose titles suggest they have personal import for me. As a writer, I need to work hard at creating titles that tap many readers on the shoulder and say: "Stop! Here's something for *you!*"

Some kinds of titles that often have strong reader appeal are:

striking statements, exclamations, direct quotations, and questions. Even a simple declarative phrase may be arresting if it has rhythm or alliteration. Whatever its form, the title should be phrased to make readers want to find out what's in the article it introduces.

PLACEMENT OF MATERIAL—OR "MARKETING"

Never overlook this crucial step toward publication: actual selling of a manuscript to a specific publisher, or "market."

Many good writers are poor salesmen of their goods. That is one reason New York and a few other cities provide work for several hundred authors' representatives, or literary agents. Except for those who actually make their living by charging "reading fees" while ostensibly centering upon fees from their sales to editors, agents have little time for a beginning writer. Nor do they have much to offer.

Unless you're convinced you have a major literary work and have personal contact with a reputable agent, steer clear of these middlemen until you have a respectable record of sales. Even then, you are likely to find that direct submissions from you to editors will give you more satisfaction than agency representation. That is especially the case if your material is selling regularly to low- and middle-pay markets. Since his 10 per cent fee on such sales can't possibly amount to much, the agent must concentrate upon top-pay markets.

Operating from your own parsonage or manse, you can place nearly all your good material . . . if you'll work at marketing with the same zeal and imagination you apply to your writing. Always remember that the production of a manuscript is only one of two crucial steps. *Until it is submitted to one editor after another, an article or feature or book has no more chance of publication than it would have had it never been written.* A work of genius lying in your desk drawer will never fire the minds and hearts of the readers for whom you produced it.

Marketing requires—and deserves—as much enthusiasm as

writing. Because it has its own set of complex variables, this side of the writer's career can be as intriguing and rewarding as translation of ideas into words.

Physical Preparation of Manuscripts

Use a good grade of white typewriter paper, size $8\frac{1}{2}''$ x 11". Type your material, double spaced, using a clear black ribbon. Write on one side of the paper only.

Place the title about halfway down the first page, with your name centered below the title. Leave ample margins at sides and bottom—about $1\frac{1}{2}''$.

On each page after the first, write the title (or an abbreviation of it) and the page number of the manuscript. Leave at least an inch margin at the top of each sheet.

Avoid trying to catch an editor's eye by means of colored paper or typewriter ribbon, decorations, or other embellishments. These devices are the mark of the amateur. Editors naturally want to see manuscripts that are easy to read, and neatness probably has some influence upon initial reaction to a piece. But their decisions are reached on the basis of whether or not the *words* of a given story fill their needs. Gimmicks designed to make a piece stand out from other material received that day are useless if not actually detrimental.

Some writers place return addresses upon the first pages of manuscripts, and do not include a covering letter. Ministers are comparatively mobile, and old manuscripts that show addresses have to be re-typed after every move. That's one reason I recommend leaving your address off manuscripts, and sending a note with each one submitted. Such a memo can be very brief unless there are special circumstances, such as availability of photos not submitted with the manuscript.

Along with your manuscript, enclose a return envelope that is stamped and fully addressed. A few major magazines send back unsolicited contributions that lack return envelopes, but most editors throw such material away. (That policy is stipulated on the contents pages of many publications.)

Do not staple your manuscripts; editors prefer to handle loose sheets. It isn't even necessary to use paper clips. If every page bears identification, there's little danger that anything will be lost. Besides, paper clips bend and score typewriter paper and give a much-traveled look to a manuscript that has been submitted only three or four times.

It's entirely in order, though, to offer material that shows some wear and tear from journeys in the mail. Publishers who buy unsolicited contributions are accustomed to the fact that "one editor's poison is another editor's bread and butter." It isn't necessarily a reflection on the quality of a story, or the judgment of an author, when an offering brings one or more rejections. A piece turned down last week by one editor, may be just what another is seeking this week. Retype your manuscripts when they begin to look badly rumpled, but not at the first appearance of a crease.

Slanting to Specific Audiences

Earlier, I pointed out that it is impossible to prepare an article or book addressed to mankind in general. Always, a manuscript must be directed to some segment of mankind. To the degree that this slice of humanity has clear traits the writer recognizes, he can "slant" his material to his readers.

First-grade children, for example, constitute an audience whose members can't possibly be reached if the writer addresses them as he would the faculty of a theological seminary. For youngsters, slanting involves the choice of brief words likely to be in their vocabulary and the selection of plot material close to their interests.

Exactly the same criteria apply to other audiences. It's a waste of time to bother editors of *The Christian Family* with a manuscript that is tailored to reading levels of those who follow the *Hibbert Journal*. Nor is there the slightest use to get a wonderful idea for a challenge directed to readers of *The Chap-*

lain, then submit it for possible publication in *Sunday School at Home.*

Choice of these farfetched examples was deliberate.

You know, of course, that as a reader you have strong preferences for some magazines and mild ones for others. If you cared to do so, you could list several characteristics of many or all persons who read these publications regularly.

In order to develop skill in marketing your manuscripts, you have only to make formal application of principles you have acquired informally, as a reader. That is, try to know as many publications as intimately as possible. Seek to understand who subscribes to each magazine on your list, and why. From time to time, forage past the borders familiar to you as a reader and investigate both individual titles and whole classes of magazines you've never known.

Some professional tools are indispensable here.

One such tool is a representative collection of contemporary magazines. You'll find it in your nearest public library of any size. If you live in or near a city with 100,000 population, local librarians will introduce you to magazines whose names you've never heard—but toward which you feel some degree of affinity. Should it be impossible for you to make periodic visits to a good library, you'll find it helpful to browse at the best newsstand you can find.

Mergers and business failures are continually thinning the ranks of magazines, while new groups of consumers and readers are creating bases for fresh ventures. Some impression of major trends can be gained from an hour a month at a magazine stand. It isn't enough, though, to jot down a memo about changes in titles published. To write for any magazine, you need to read it until you have at least a general impression of major subjects covered and the style of writing that is used.

Published aids for writers are as important as firsthand familiarity with markets. These aids take two forms: periodic listing of editorial requirements in books slanted to free lances, and month-by-month reports plus how-to-do-it articles in writers' magazines.

You will find it essential to buy and use at least one market guide, and at least one monthly magazine.

The Writer's Handbook, issued annually, lists several hundred magazine and book publishers. It may be ordered through your local bookstore or directly from *The Writer,* Inc., Boston, Mass. *Writer's Market,* revised at intervals of about six months, describes some 2500 markets for free-lance writers. It may be secured from publishers of *Writer's Digest,* Cincinnati 10, Ohio.

Half a dozen magazines are tailored to special interests of free-lance writers. They offer late news about changes in editorial needs and rates, plus articles of advice by writers and editors. Three of these magazines are especially useful: *Author & Journalist, The Writer,* and *Writer's Digest.* Buy sample copies at your newsstand to become acquainted with them; then subscribe to and faithfully read at least one.

Through your book which lists markets, and your magazine reports about current trends, you will gradually extend your knowledge of the publishing field. From time to time, you'll learn of a magazine that sounds interesting—one for which you'd like to write. In such cases, most editors will send a few copies of back issues if you'll explain your interest and send postage.

If you have a working knowledge of only a dozen magazines —about the extent of the average minister's consistent reading—you probably find yourself defeated every time you get a rejection. It has come from the editor whom you hoped to please; now you have nowhere else to send your story.

Multiply your market knowledge only ten times—to about 120 magazines—and your chances of selling may be multiplied 100 times. For instead of having only one potential market for a given manuscript, you are likely to have a dozen or twenty. Like skill in writing techniques, knowledge of marketing can be acquired gradually over a period of time. If you'll apply to it the same hard work and alert intelligence you use in sharpening your skill as a communicator, your market sense will mature along with your literary craftsmanship.

Planning and Persistence

Begin now—today—the practice of making a "marketing card" or routing slip for the manuscript most recently completed. On that card, list the title of your piece, audience for whom it was written, and approximate length. Then select all the magazines that can be found whose editors need material of that sort in the length you've employed.

On your marketing card, list these magazines in the order of their importance to you. Before you submit your manuscript for a first reading, make up your mind that you will offer it in turn to every editor on your card, until someone buys it. Do the same thing with book manuscripts.

How long should you continue to submit rejected material?

As long as you have the slightest faith in it. Persistence is fully as important as planning. You will have wasted your time in getting acquainted with a big group of markets and selecting those that seem most likely for a given manuscript, unless you follow through to the end.

My own most unusual experience of this sort was with a story of courage in everyday life. At the time I wrote my piece, *Coronet* was using one-page hero stories. Editors had bought two or three such pieces from me; the latest seemed a natural for the series. But instead of packing it off to *Coronet* without a second thought, I listed about twenty magazines that seemed potential markets for the piece.

My story was in the mail only a few days, the first trip. *Coronet* editors had a full inventory, so didn't even hold my manuscript the usual thirty days. It went down my list, one magazine at a time, until it reached the bottom. Submitted to *Swing*, the house magazine of a western radio station, it was held there for three or four months. Finally I became impatient and asked that the piece be returned.

It had been re-typed three or four times; damage to the most recent typescript was slight. So I faced a dilemma. Here was a manuscript that I still regarded as a good story of its kind . . . and there was no place to send it. Or was there? I could start over at the beginning and repeat the cycle of submissions that began two years earlier. That's what I decided to do; on its second trip to *Coronet,* the piece won quick acceptance.

Bizarre? Yes—but only in degree. Except for full-time professional writers and free lances who have made a name in some specialization, most writers receive a stream of rejection slips. Though persistence in marketing won't make up for substandard writing, it will go a long way to raise one's ratio of acceptances. Instead of being unusual, it is commonplace for even writers of some standing to place material after three or four or ten submissions rather than one.

Plan, therefore, and persist.

Get fully acquainted with as many markets as possible. Look at every manuscript in terms of a list of editors who might like it. Then keep that manuscript in the mail until it wears out. If you still have faith in the piece, re-type it and keep trying.

Never throw away an article or feature or book in which you have any degree of confidence; never invest hours or days in a manuscript and then stop trying to place it after devoting a few minutes to marketing. If you believe in your writing enough to give it some of your own "blood, sweat, and tears," then by all means be equally zealous at the other half of the writer's task: marketing.

GRATIS WORK FOR NEWS PUBLICATIONS

Even though no payment is involved, it is customary to speak of a medium of publication as a "market." This terminology helps create consciousness that a manuscript is a commodity whose submission to an editor is a business transaction. Acceptance or rejection has no more connotation of editorial bias (favorable or unfavorable) than does a merchant's agreement or refusal to purchase goods from a manufacturer.

Daily and weekly newspapers, along with denominational news publications of state or regional circulation, make up an important market for the religion writer. Except in the case of a metropolitan daily paper that uses a feature column on continuing basis, these media do not pay for material. That being the case, it would seem that such papers have their doors wide open to potential writers.

It isn't that simple. Even gratis work for papers of low circulation has its problems. No editor can give space to material that doesn't fit the working philosophy of his paper. Though he himself may be greatly interested in sermons, he's unlikely to publish one each week unless readers share that interest. Material that is far off the beaten path has to be superlatively good in order to get consideration.

Again, editors of both religious and secular news publications are deluged with religious material. Most of it is so poor it can be rejected at a glance. Still, the sheer volume of such copy constitutes a hurdle.

Like every other barrier, these can be overcome. Be patient in producing and submitting manuscripts of professional quality. You can be sure that sooner or later one or more editors will use your work.

When you once break through, you'll find great satisfaction from seeing your words in print. Nothing I ever wrote gave me more pleasure than a column called "Nuggets From My Notebook." As pastor of a three-church rural charge, I wrote the weekly piece gratis—and was paid liberally by seeing it appear in *The South Carolina Methodist Advocate*. No matter how obscure the publication that uses your work, it will take your ideas to a bigger audience than most men face from the pulpit. You may write prayers, Bible vignettes, devotions, or other such material for years and never receive a dollar. But you'll be paid generously in satisfaction and sense of achievement.

Many ministers have found no-pay markets to constitute their most gratifying field for self-expression and Christian witness. If you've seriously considered writing, select this or another category of markets and get busy in a disciplined program of manuscript production—today.

Come on in . . . the water's fine!

3

So You Want To Write a Book

FRANK S. MEAD

So YOU WANT to write a book?

Welcome to the fraternity; we extend to you the writing hand of fellowship and wish you well as you enter the vale of toil, sweat and tears. You are about to engage in the most exasperating and exacting and satisfying effort to which you can put your time, mind and hand and, as the editor said when he rejected the author's manuscript for the fifth time, "If there is anything I can do to help you. . . ."

Perhaps we can help most by suggesting that you ask yourself three questions before you take the plunge. It is no news that the competent and trained newspaper reporter asks himself six questions before he writes his lead paragraph—the "Sacred Six" of the fourth estate—Who? What? Where? When? How? Why? For the purpose you have in mind—the writing of a book—reduce them to three—Why? What? How?

WHY?

Why do you want to write a book? What drives you?

Most preachers write books because they have something to say that they (or a publisher) think worthy of saying to the largest possible audience—a perfectly legitimate drive and desire. Jesus went out to talk to "multitudes" on a mountainside when there was no hall or synagogue large enough to hold them, and to write a book for a multitude is quite as logical and realistic. Many preachers have found outlets for their preaching in books that they could never have found behind a pulpit. Lloyd Douglas reached better than 800,000 with his *Magnificent*

Obsession, more than two million with *The Robe,* and in those books millions who never go to church saw the face of Jesus Christ.

Religious best-sellers are written because their authors have to write them—and not for cash. If you are thinking of writing as one way to make a fortune, forget it. James Michener, who has been on more than one best-seller list, tells us that he barely made expenses until he wrote *Hawaii.* Carl Sandburg nearly starved to death until he "clicked" with his immortal work on Lincoln. Two topflight novelists collaborated for nearly ten years on a recent book of fiction; it made a best seller and a movie, but after paying living expenses (you have to live while you're writing!) and income tax, they figured they had cleared $400 per person per year for their labors. There may be a half-dozen big-time writers in the United States who support themselves by full-time writing; the rest support themselves as editors, mechanics, movie actors—or preachers.

Of course, any minister worthy of his calling knows all this, and agrees. It is an old axiom in the preaching guild that he who preaches for money or economic security has found the shortest road to hell; likewise, the writer who writes *only* for pay has found an alternate route. The finest minister-authors we know pay little attention to their royalty checks; *they write because God drives them to write.* The stimulus for writing a book must ultimately be the same as the stimulus for preaching a sermon: "This is something that must be said; I cannot but speak."

You'll probably never get rich with your book, but you can realize the exhilaration of watching your idea become a book, and you can reach thousands with your pen where you could reach only hundreds with your voice. Money is a by-product of this art, as it is in all the arts; the real reward comes in contributing something of real value to people who need it.

Or you may want to do it because someone who likes you or your preaching tells you that you ought to write a book. Every editor, every day of his miserable life, gets a letter from some embryo author who says, "I showed this to one of my best friends, and *he* says it ought to be published." Of course. A friend is a friend, and he doesn't want to hurt you by telling you it's no good or just so-so. He wants to encourage you; he might be doing you a real favor if he discouraged you. There are times when your best friend can be your worst enemy, and this is one of them. *He* may say he likes what you have written because he likes you—but how many will like it who have never seen or heard of you, and probably never will? What interests him—or you—may interest few others, if any. Don't go into a sulk or wear your heart on your sleeve when the editor informs you that your friend may like it, but he doesn't. The editor has to ask himself, "How many people would think enough of this to put down $2.50 or $3.00 of their hard-earned cash to buy it?" You have only one critic in your friend, and a prejudiced critic at that; when you put your name on a book and put that book in the bookstores, you invite the criticism of thousands who are not so sympathetic; you are suddenly a Daniel in a literary lion's den. They are all from Missouri; they have to be shown that what you have to say is worth saying and worth reading. They are merciless; they can rend you limb from limb. In His providence, the Almighty has created editors to save the innocent from such fate.

We know some who write *only* to get their names into print. May we humbly suggest that there are easier ways of doing this —like shooting a deacon or sitting on a pillar in the town square. Dorothy Parker said once, "The writer's way is rough and lonely, and who would choose it while there are vacancies in more gracious professions such as, say, cleaning out ferryboats?"

But if you have that burning coal from God upon your lips or heart; if deep within there is that seething of the spirit which must be expressed and broadcast that more and more may hear and know; if there is that sense of truth, mercy, love and justice which has been too long denied and upon which you are equipped of God to throw new light; if you can open a window on truth which no one else has yet opened; if you can say it better than it has yet been said; if you have the rare talent of putting truth into singing words; if an editor or publisher writes, "I believe this should be published . . ."; if not one friend but any considerable number of strangers say, "I wish I had that in print" . . . *then write it.*

Good books have such urgency behind them. Dr. Johnson may have written *Rasselas* to pay the expenses of his mother's funeral and her debts, and he may have said that anyone who writes for anything but money is a fool, but it still holds that *Rasselas* was written out of one of the deepest spiritual struggles the choleric Doctor ever knew, and therefore remains one of the best things he ever wrote. Zola was at his best in writing his thunderous philippics in defense of Captain Dreyfus; John Bunyan wrote *Pilgrim's Progress* because he had to write it— an overwhelming conviction rent his heart and filled his mind and he *had* to give it to mankind. Walter Rauschenbusch and Reinhold Niebuhr saw so much of human pain and insecurity and social and economic oppression that they *had* to write their famous books in defense of those who suffered in the midst of abundance. Dale Evans Rogers will hoot at being set in such company, but she did write in *Angel Unaware* a message on the death of her baby that has captured the hearts of tens of thousands.

We like the old painter who explained the success of his paintings: "Before beginning my work, I wait until all thought of fame which this might bring is gone from my mind. Then I wait a little longer, until all thought of money is gone. Finally, I wait until all thought of self is gone. After that, I know that I am ready to begin painting."

Write to meet a need. You will not need to hunt long to find a need; just talk with your neighbor or walk down the street or read your newspaper or ask your congregation why they come to church. Needs are a dime a dozen; books that competently and honestly get down to the business of meeting those needs are hard to find. The door is wide open for *your* book!

WHAT?

Having decided why you should write—*what* should you
write? We once heard Senator Beveridge of Indiana say to a
college audience, in a speech on speech-making, "Never get up
to make a speech unless you have something to say." It was
Thoreau who said, on being told that a cable had been laid on
the floor of the ocean between England and America, "Very
good. Now I suppose the first news to come over it will be that
Princess Adelaid has the measles." That is the rub: what will
you say, what will you write? You can write either sense or non-
sense (both seem to sell well, at times), and there are several
ways of doing it.

One is just to sit down and write what you feel like writing,
without consulting anybody. That is good exercise, and you will
need a lot of exercise in writing, but don't expect very much of
it to be published. One of the saddest duties of any editor comes
when he has to reject a manuscript which has taken the author
anywhere from one year to five years to write, but which is of
no interest whatever to anyone but the author. We recently received a weighty tome in which the author, proceeding from
"newly discovered evidence" which he somehow failed to produce, tried to prove that Jesus was university-educated and a
world-traveler. He had spent two years of his life dealing spec-
ulatively with something on which there was no historical evidence whatever, to write something that hardly a baker's dozen
would care to read. He was completely fascinated by his subject, and buoyantly certain that it would sell a million copies,
but for the life of him the editor couldn't sense any enthusiasm
for that one, so back it went. A few scholars and teachers and
curious seekers after the unimportant just *might* have read it,
but the publisher who publishes for the few doesn't stay a publisher very long; that way lies suicide, and he knows it, even
though the author doesn't. Don't waste your time!

Keep your eye on two individuals, when you sit down to
write: yourself, and the man you want to read your book. You

may want to prove something or other; be sure that reader is interested in seeing you prove it. Was it Dr. McCracken who said recently that the trouble with too many preachers right now was that they seemed intent on answering questions nobody asks?

Find out what questions they are asking, before you offer your answers in type. Find out what publishers are publishing; they will be glad to send you their catalogues. But be warned: do *not* try to fit yourself, as a round peg in a square hole, into any publisher's list unless you can write with authority in one or another of the areas in which he publishes. Some houses are doing very well right now with books on sex and the Beatnicks —can you write about that, or them? *Should* you? There is an interest in books on Zen Buddhism—but you are probably the last man in the world to write about *that*. Stick to your last. Write in your field. Don't go jumping fences into other, strange fields where you'll get lost and look ridiculous. We know a *few* ministers who try to write on everything from the care and feeding of centipedes to the floor plan of the seventh heaven beyond the seventh heaven. They write, but they do not publish.

Remember, too, that public taste is fickle, and changeable without advance notice. A few years ago you could find any best-seller list well stocked with religious books; on one before us as we write, published this week, we find just one religious book—the New English Bible. Today people want to read about the Civil War; any seventh-grade schoolboy can write on the War Between the States, and get it published (it would be interesting to know how well most of these Civil War books really *sell*); tomorrow it may be the Revolution or the Punic Wars or Martin Luther or Charlemagne—who knows? Yesterday peace of mind books were selling like popcorn at a county fair; today most of us seem to have decided that we aren't going to have any peace of mind for some time to come, and probably *shouldn't* have it, so we aren't buying those books any more.

Know what they want—yes—but do not cater to a whim. Write for tomorrow, not today. The fact that the New English

Bible is the only survivor on that best-seller list is worth a second thought: the Bible was written for tomorrow, and tomorrow, and tomorrow. There have been millions of books written on passing religious fads since Guttenberg put his first Scriptures on the press; just try and find them now!

The most sensible way to start writing your book, and to determine what you should write, is to query an editor about it before you even sharpen your pencil. When you're sick you consult a doctor, and if you are possessed of any intelligence at all you accept his advice as advice from one who knows. When you get all tangled up in your income-tax report, you consult a tax expert, and you follow his counsel. You can save yourself a lot of time and grief by simply writing an editor, or sitting down with him if he is near your home, telling him about your idea, what you want to do and how you intend to do it. (If you write, *please* don't say, "I have a manuscript I would like you to publish. . . !" Give him details—on content, approach, background, even on the number of words in your manuscript, if you expect him to nibble.) You can do the same thing through a literary agent, but agents cost money, and few of them are interested in religious writing. The editor will be the final judge of your job anyway, so get to him first. Don't sit up nights for five years laboring over something that no editor in his right mind will even read; don't send it off "cold" to the editor or publisher. Let him know it is coming; if you don't, your masterpiece will be only one more in the everlasting pile of manuscripts on his desk, and it is quite possible that as such it will get a too-hasty examination. (Editors do have bad days, when they shouldn't be reading manuscripts at all.) We call these "over-the-transom" manuscripts, and most of them go right back over the transom, pronto. Some publishers may not read them at all; they work out their ideas for books with their authors, and are tempted to ignore unsolicited or undiscussed manuscripts. But when the editor knows your manuscript is coming to his desk because he has encouraged you to write it and send it, there is at least a faint "welcome" on his editorial door mat.

The manuscripts that come to his desk fall naturally into certain categories, for the very simple reason that there are only certain fields in which the minister can or should write. First of all, there are sermons. Most books written by preachers started as preaching, and every other preacher in the United States wants to publish those sermons. Some should, and some should not. *If* the sermon has a new approach or a fresh insight, *if* it has an arresting application to life, if it is said better than the run-of-the-mine sermon says it, then it has a good chance; lacking that, it is a poor publishing risk.

For instance—we have before us a manuscript of sermons, and the first sermon starts with the line, "Communism is the curse of the modern world, and the most determined enemy of Christianity." That is the sort of opening that puts the editor to sleep—or in a tantrum. He *knows* that, and so do the poor long-suffering laymen; they have been told that ten thousand times, and they are weary of hearing it, and they know what the preacher is going to say before he says it, and they don't much care. Contrast that with the opening sentence of a sermon by Peter Marshall, preached back in the days when the country was first rocked by the revelations of a Kefauver Congressional investigating committee: "How would you like to be on an investigating committee . . . to inquire into the qualifications of those who sought to be disciples of Jesus?" We read that one twice, then read the sermon, then published it in a book called *Mr. Jones Meet the Master*—the most widely read book of sermons in modern times—perhaps *ever* read. This approach was fresh, unique: the preacher picked up the layman and put him up there on the bench with the investigators; it gave the layman credit for being both an intelligent man *and* a disciple, and it shocked him into thinking, "I wonder if *I* have the qualifications. . . ?" This is getting our reader with the first line; if you do not get him with the first line, you probably will never get him at all.

"Oh, sure, you published Peter Marshall," says the cynic. "He was famous, and the famous get published, and the little fellow hasn't a chance." No, he wasn't famous. He had never published a book, before *Mr. Jones.* He was published not because he was famous, but because he had verve and style and originality and imagination and something to say that had never been said that way before. (Notice the surprising arrangement of material in his sermons; that nonconformity in structure sold thousands of his book.) It is not true that only the "big-shot" preacher has a chance at publication. What did you know about Rabbi Liebman before he wrote *Peace of Mind?* Or of a Lutheran parson named Lloyd Douglas before he wrote *The Magnificent Obsession?* But it *is* true that the preacher who will really work to say it well, and who will pay the price in writing and rewriting, has a good chance. Even Shakespeare started as an unknown.

It should be understood that a *lot* of rewriting is necessary, for a sermon preached from a pulpit is one thing and a sermon in cold print is quite another. Phillips Brooks described preaching as, "Truth mediated through personality." The personality is present in the pulpit; it is missing in the book, and you must compensate for the missing personality with better-than-average writing. That takes a lot of midnight oil—or early rising.

A miscellaneous collection of unrelated sermons *may* interest this larger congregation of book readers; if it is a collection of rewritten sermons built around a central theme or idea, it is much more likely to hold them. Dr. J. Wallace Hamilton is one of the most popular authors in this field; his *Ride the Wild Horses* was originally a series of sermons dealing with the use of our human instincts and emotions in abundant spiritual living, and his other books began the same way—and he labored mightily in changing the sermons into chapters, in cutting out the old stereotyped homiletic references and emphases. He *made it over* into an "idea" book, with the idea flowing smoothly from start to finish. Rabbi Liebman did the same thing with *Peace of Mind,* and Norman Vincent Peale's books reflect his preaching. Yet as they have appeared in book form, these pulpit messages are quite different from the original discourses; they have had the benefit of meticulous editing, rewriting and rephrasing, by both author and editor, and *that* makes them good reading.

On the other hand (if the Methodists and the Wesleyans will forgive me for saying it) the sermons of John Wesley which we read today are *not* good reading, for the simple reason that too many editors have had their hands in the broth, and spoiled it; they have left in those sermons much that should have been cut, for book purposes, and they have taken out of them what must have been the really lively portions that shook England and saved her from a British imitation of the French Revolution. It is difficult to believe that the immortal Wesley ever preached those sermons as we have them now, or that the mobs threw rocks at him in the streets of Bristol for preaching them. It takes time, talent and a great deal of sympathetic teamwork between author and editor to make a sermon readable.

It might just be that you should write something other than sermons. Emphasis on preaching seems to have given over, in our theological schools, to emphasis on counseling and administration, and books of sermons, frankly, are not as popular as they were twenty years ago. You might do a book on church administration—*if* you are an administrator; there is a definite increase in interest in such books. If you try this, make it human, not academic. Don't *preach* administration; tell them *how*. That word "How" in a book is as valuable as a Scotch accent in a Presbyterian preacher. People in the churches want to know how—how to run a Sunday school, build a church, furnish and decorate it, how to cook for crowds, how to be a good usher, how to conduct a building or financial campaign. . . .

Approach a book on counseling from the same human standpoint; read everything you can get your hands on, here, before venturing into the field, for a great deal is being written and written well by experts. Some of them are *too* expert, sacrificing personality for professionalism. Write with your eye on the layman; after all, he is the ultimate consumer in counseling, the beginning and the end of it all, and the book should be written to help him as much as the counselor. Christian counseling is as old as its Founder; we sometimes wonder why more attention is not paid in our modern "counseling method" books to the method of that Founder.

Many preachers want to publish columns they have written for newspapers or magazines. "These columns have been very popular in our little newspaper in Perkin's Corners (population 1200) and many of my readers have been asking for them in book form. I know they would sell. . . ." Maybe. But what goes over well in Perkin's Corners may fall very, very flat in Philadelphia, and Philadelphia sells more books in a day than Perkin's Corners sells in five years. This is another way of saying that the material in your column *must* have national interest if it is to be circulated nationally, in a book. Be sure it has that; no publisher will risk his money on a book that is wanted only in Perkin's Corners.

If they have something for people in Seattle as well as in New York, the publisher may like them—*if* they are carefully "slanted" or made readable for that larger audience. One of the top writers in the religious field has published several very successful books based on his newspaper columns; but his material was first preached from the pulpit, then rewritten for the newspaper column, then rewritten a *third* time for his books. Those books sell.

Whatever you do, do *not* paste up your columns and send them to the publisher, as is; unless they have the mark of genius, they will be returned in the next mail. To the publisher, they are "cold turkey"—food already offered to a comparatively small audience and read by a comparative few who will *not* spend two or three dollars for the privilege of reading them again.

Devotions? Books of devotions—especially books of prayers —are increasingly popular. The demand is not for books of devotional material filched from St. Francis of Assisi or John Donne, but for devotions and prayers that have burst out of the writer's own heart—original, pertinent, thought-out and wrought-out prayers that deal with life as we know it now.

Write either for individuals or for groups; don't try to write for both in the same book (it is done now and then, but rarely). It is far better to specialize, to write for teen-agers, or for young adults, or for men, or for women. Youth, for instance, has a language—and problems—all its own; a book slanted at adults will not interest them. Shun verbosity. The man who said that a preacher who couldn't say what he had to say in twenty minutes would never say it had something—and it goes for praying as well as preaching. If you "pray around the world" in a book of printed prayers, for everyone from the Statue of Liberty to the Taj Mahal, effusively, endlessly, your book will die on the bookstands. Study the needs of those to whom you offer your prayers and devotions—as the Quakers put it, "Speak to their condition."

Church groups are asking for more and better devotional services in book form. They want complete, *short* devotional outlines and services usable by groups of men, women, children, young people. Give it to them in short, condensed form. Suggest hymns they might use, but do not write out the hymns; they have hymnals available. Give them appropriate Scriptural references, but do not take up valuable space in your book in writing out the Scripture; they have Bibles. Use your space to give them good readable narrative material, illustrations, word pictures, leads. And do *not* ask them to go downtown to the public library for a dozen books that will give them "additional material"; nine-tenths of them will never go.

Fiction? The publishers are looking desperately for good religious fiction. Not that there is any lack of manuscripts; fiction is a flood that pours over the editor's desk every morning with the nine o'clock mail. But *good* fiction—that's something else. The trouble with (all) fiction, says Norman Cousins, is that it is about people not worth knowing—or people worth knowing who suffer badly at the hands of the inexperienced writer. Fiction is a high art; it is one of the most difficult of all writing mediums, and it calls for a built-in or born-in talent. Lloyd Douglas was a pastor *and* a born storyteller, and he left the pulpit to write religious fiction. A. J. Cronin (*Keys of the Kingdom*) quit medicine to become a novelist. Charles Kingsley wrote great novels in his day, but Kingsley remained a small-town preacher to the end of his days, with time to put on his writing. It takes time—a lot of time, a lifetime. Try it, if you have the gift. But bring something new in your basket; don't just tell the story of some Bible character all over again, as it has been told since the first Bible was printed. Read Sholem Asch, or Frank Slaughter; see how *they* tell those stories, and go and do likewise. The demand is great, and increasing; the mantles of Asch, Douglas and Cronin are waiting for strong shoulders to wear them.

Poetry? No. Nine times out of ten, no. Not, at least, for profit. The best of publishers have a hard time of it selling the best of poets; it is disgraceful but it is true that most poets starve and die unhonored and unread. Now and then we get a manuscript of poetry that makes us sit up in our editorial chair, but even then the inevitable question comes: *"You* like it, because you like good poetry—but how many will buy it?" Of course, if you *must* write poetry, you will write it, market or no market; that urge is no more to be denied than the urge to preach. But write it for the lifting up of your mind and soul, and not to sell. The market simply isn't there, especially for *religious* poetry. How many preachers do you know who publish verse? Or who use it, to any great extent, in their preaching?

Books on healing are in demand. This may be due to the fact that the churches have been making a real effort to elevate standards in healing, and to take it out of the hands of those charlatans who heal for a price and catch the next train out of town. Some fine and substantial books are being written, by men and women who know whereof they speak; some of the best minds in the church are at work in this area. The best of them are writing books filled not with exhortation but with actual case histories, proved methods and examples. The public is wary of books on healing which are completely devoted to remote and unattested miracles; they are reading books written by reliable and successful practitioners—and there are plenty of such practitioners available to the serious writer.

Books of sermon illustrations always have a good potential; ministers are begging for such material, and it is nothing less than criminal that they are too often driven to the newspapers and secular magazines in their search for it. The popular books here are not padded with the old, hackneyed stories about George Washington or David Livingstone which we heard when we were children in Sunday school; they have a content as lively and up-to-date as your morning paper. If you will take the time to mark and copy the unusual sparkling stories and illustrations you read in your books, periodicals and newspapers, and add to them a "punch line" of Christian emphasis or application, you will have something every editor in America will want. Beware of the stilted and the stale. There is a gold mine of material available here for the preacher with a little imagination, and it is being tossed into the wastebasket every hour of the day.

If you write on doctrine or theological themes, you write for a divided market. Such books *must* be written, and always will be, but generally speaking they are written for one or another of our churches or schools of theology. Those who agree with you will buy such books; those who do not, will not, unless you happen to be a Barth or a Niebuhr. The seminaries of your denomination, Bible schools and colleges, institutes, teachers, students, preachers—these, and not the laymen—are your readers. Your denominational publishing house is probably your best outlet, in this department of writing.

Some good books on perfectly good themes go begging in the bookstores, because of circumstances beyond anyone's control. Books on missions and missionaries sold widely, just a few years back; today they are hard to sell. If your story is as good as the recent *Gates of Splendor* or *Beyond Cotabato,* or as important or dramatic as the stories of Albert Schweitzer and Frank Laubach, any publisher will be interested. Such missionary books find widespread enthusiasm across denominational lines. *The*

Nun's Story, with a Roman Catholic sister as heroine, was read by thousands of Protestants, and Roman Catholics read Laubach. The popularity of such books may be an indication of a new direction in missions, and an awareness of these new directions should be well rooted in the mind of anyone writing in the field.

New translations of the Scriptures continue to sell well when authoritatively done—usually by groups of recognized scholars. J. B. Phillips and James Moffatt's translations done by individuals, are exceptions that prove the rule. Translations by a single author find it tough going. There is a feeling among the publishers that there may be a sudden reaction, as the market becomes saturated with "new" translations, and that the confused public will turn back to the King James. Working out a translation takes years of hard labor; ask a publisher about it, before going too far.

Some seasonal books—written, for instance, for Christmas or Easter—do well. They must do well in a very short space of time; once Christmas or Easter are gone, such books die quickly. Nobody buys a Christmas book in January or July! They should not be too short—not less than 150-200 pages—for smaller books bearing a smaller price must be printed in much larger editions if they are to pay production costs; the paperbacks you see in your drugstore are printed in lots of 50,000 to 100,000 and up, and few religious books sell in such quantity. They must be unusually well done, and circulated quickly—and then forgotten. Not one in ten thousand of them is offered for sale the *next* Christmas or Easter.

You have a thesis written in college or theological school, for your master's or doctor's degree? These, generally, are of more interest to the students who *had* to write them and the poor faculty members who *had* to read them, than to the average layman, and they call for drastic reworking and rewording if they are to reach the common reader. The "thesis curse" must be cut out, and the highly technical or academic language and emphases. It can and has been done; William M. Ramsay currently has an excellent book in *The Christ of the Earliest Christians,* which was originally a Ph.D. thesis written at Edinburgh, and which he popularized for the Church audience. If you will not sweat to get it down where the layman can read it and understand it—please, brother, *keep* it!

HOW?

Just *how* do you go about writing your book and getting it published?

For some, it seems no effort at all; they simply have their secretaries (if they are lucky enough to have one of those) or their typing wives (if they are lucky enough to have married one) type off a dozen or so of their sermons and mail them off to the publisher. Believe it or not, it sometimes works! Harper's editors tell us that when a manuscript comes in from Dr. Harry Emerson Fosdick, it is so good, and in such a state of perfection, that it can be sent off to the printer without so much as a casual glance from a copy-editor. But no man in America works harder over his sermons or books than Dr. Fosdick; those manuscripts have years of work behind them before they reach Harper's editors.

Most preachers will have to go at it another way. They will have to get up early and work late. A French statesman says that the Germans have won their two out of three modern wars with the French by getting up an hour earlier every morning. It makes sense—for writers as well as for German soldiers. Getting at it early in the day means that you are getting at it when your mind is fresh and clear. Set aside the early morning hours for so much writing every day, and *stick to it.* The man who does his writing in his odd moments produces an odd book.

You may have to force yourself to do it, but you will not be an odd fellow in that; most writers have to force themselves to get down to work, every day of their lives. Anatole France, in his fine mature years of writing, used to throw himself on the floor and kick his heels in the air, like a spoiled child, when it came time for him to write; if it had not been for a stout-hearted Madame France, there would have been no famous Anatole. Get at it early and stick at it, on a regular daily schedule. If you can, get a hideaway somewhere, to which you can retreat from telephone bells and noisy neighbors, and concentrate, and write even though you never publish a word of it. Booth Tarkington wrote for seven years before he sold a line. William Allen White used to say that writers were never born but made through the daily application of the seat of the writer to the seat of a chair. When a young hopeful wrote to Leonard Merrick asking, "Is there any single piece of advice you would care to give to a young man about to embark on a literary career?" Merrick wrote back, "I will give you not only the best, but the only piece of advice I possess. Here it is: Write, write, write, write, write, write. . . ." The whole page of the letter was filled with that one word, *"write."*

Before you write, *think*. Meditate. Let your idea "perk" in your mind for weeks, months, before you set pen to paper or ribbon in typewriter. (And please start with a *new* ribbon!) Kipling was once asked how he was coming along with a new book, and he said, "Fine. I've got it all down in my head; now all I need to do is to get it down on paper." William Faulkner said he just sat down and listened to his voices, and then wrote what they said, and never changed it, because the voices were always right. Listen before you write.

When it comes clear, outline it. Writing is like filling in the spaces between your fingers; you get the main points clear, then fill in the details you have worked out in your research. An outline to a writer is as important as a map to a traveler; you have to know exactly where you're going. It is essential to clarity and to the orderly progress of your writing. A good editor can tell in five minutes flat whether you have just written it "off the top of your head" or whether you have built it with the conscience of a good bricklayer. Never let the outline "develop" as you write; it will *not* develop in time to save you; you will forget things you meant to say and say a lot of things you never meant to say, and there will be no health in you or your manuscript. Put more than you will need into this outline; it is easier to cut than to add, and it is always better to have too much than too little, at the beginning. Think of what John Mark had to write about, when he began writing his Gospel— and see how mercilessly he cut and condensed it down to the barest essentials and into the most authoritative and most copied of all four Gospels! Have more than you need; then start throwing it out.

Once you get down to the actual writing, make haste slowly. Write, and rewrite. Take an hour, if you must, to get the right word in the right place; chain a dictionary to one elbow and a thesaurus to the other; you will never walk a writing mile without both. Joseph Conrad called it a good day when he wrote just one perfect sentence; Somerset Maugham settled for 1000 good words a day. Write a chapter, study it, tear it to pieces and write it again. Then give it to some good critic who will tell you the truth about it.

Learn to accept criticism; ask for it. The late inimitable William L. Stidger, who taught preaching at Boston School of Theology and wrote many a good book, sent an article to a friendly editor who had been publishing his articles for years, but who sent this one back with the words, "No, Bill, it just isn't good enough; a lot of high-school paragraphs strung together do *not* make a good article." Dr. Stidger took that letter into one of his classes next morning, and read it to his students, as a warning against sloppy work. Then he rewrote the article into one of his finest magazine pieces.

Write and cut. Cut out the repetitions, the florid purple passages. Death to the adjective, where and when it isn't needed. Dr. Roy L. Smith, still one of our topflight writers for religious books and periodicals after a quarter of a century, tells us that "Years ago an old man called my attention to a very important fact. He insisted that I should study words carefully in order to make exact use of them, and for twenty-five years I spent an average of thirty minutes every day writing epigrams. I wrote them with the utmost care so as to make sure that when I had my sentence completed, it expressed exactly what I wanted to say and in the most graphic possible language, but I worked on that thing for twenty-five years and did it as a regular chore" (*Church Management,* May, 1961). How many words do you suppose he crossed out?

At least, we can labor to say it well—*and* briefly. The unpardonable sin in preaching is apparent when the preacher takes a simple truth and drowns it in fifty-dollar words, to the point where even *he* doesn't understand it, let alone his people. We only compound the felony when we repeat it in a book. Ninety per cent of the manuscripts that are rejected are rejected because the writer is too lazy or too preoccupied to say it well and clearly. We know of only one writer of religious books who gets his work published in spite of the fact that he says the same thing fifteen times in fifteen different ways—and people buy his books not because they like his books but because they like him. Write, write, write.

Perhaps this will help you, if you are struggling with your first manuscript. Whenever the Fleming H. Revell Company discovers a new author, they give him a helping hand with the following:

A WORD TO THE AUTHOR

In order to save time and temper, may we as publishers of your proposed book offer the following suggestions concerning the manuscript you wish to submit to us?

I. *Typing*

    A. Manuscripts must be typed double-space on clean, durable, white 8½" by 11" paper, on one side only, with margins of at least one inch on all four sides.

    B. Only original (no carbon) copies are acceptable. A carbon may be requested in case the manuscript is accepted, but only first-copy originals are considered on submission.

    C. Pages are to be numbered consecutively in the upper

right-hand corner of the page, from start to finish, and
never by chapters.

II. *Front Matter*

Front matter (the material printed in the front of the
book, preceding the narrative) must be included with the
manuscript. This includes:

1. Title page, with the title of the work and the name of
   the author clearly typed.
2. Dedication, if the author wishes one.
3. Table of contents.
4. Introduction or preface.

III. *Index*

The index, or indices, must be prepared by the author
and included with the manuscript upon submission, with
manuscript page numbers, which are changed later by the
publisher when page proof is received.

IV. *Headings*

A. Special headings within chapters, either centered or to the
   side of the page, are undesirable except in the case of
   textbooks.
B. The publisher reserves the right to rearrange, alter or
   delete such headings, in the interest of creating a more
   readable and attractive page and book.

V. *Footnotes*

A. The publisher prefers to put all footnotes together at the
   end of the book or at the end of each chapter, rather than
   at the foot of each page, where they offer expensive composition and printing problems.
B. Such footnotes must be correctly marked with similar
   letters or numbers used both on the quotations in the
   narrative, and on the footnotes themselves, wherever they
   are placed.
C. A new series of numbers is to be used for each chapter.

VI. *Illustrations*

A. Where the inclusion of illustrations has been agreed upon
   between the author and the publisher, these must be in-

cluded with the manuscript. Each piece of illustration copy should be numbered on the back (*lightly,* in pencil, to avoid any damage to the side which must be reproduced) and caption copy, together with necessary credits, should be typed on a separate sheet of paper, number keyed to the illustration copy for proper identification. Photographs and drawings should be packed carefully with stiff board when mailed, since any damage, such as a fold or crack, will appear when the copy is reproduced.

B. Note that permission must be secured to use illustrations which have been published elsewhere or furnished at a fee, which fee must be paid by the author.

VII. *Spelling and Punctuation*

A. Spelling must be consistent throughout the manuscript, based upon one dictionary, preferably Merriam-Webster Unabridged or Collegiate editions, or American College Dictionary.

B. The publisher reserves the privilege of following his house style. (Revell uses the *Manual of Style* published by the University of Chicago Press.)

C. Revell capitalizes divine pronouns; viz., He, Him, His, Thee, Thy, Thou, when used in reference to God or Christ (except as they appear in quotations from the Bible). We also capitalize Kingdom of God, Kingdom of Heaven, Holy Spirit, Cross (only when it refers to Christ's Cross), Church (when it refers to a local Church or to a particular denomination), Gospel (only when it refers specifically to the Gospel of Matthew, etc.). Relative pronouns referring to the Deity are *not* capitalized (as who, whom, etc.).

D. The titles of all Bible books are to be spelled out fully, never abbreviated.

E. In punctuation, quotation marks are placed outside the comma, period, exclamation point or interrogation mark ending the sentence, except when an interrogative sentence ends in a declarative quotation, in which case the question mark is placed outside the quotation marks. In the case of double and single quotes ending a sentence, both sets of marks are placed outside the punctuation, with the exception noted above. The semi-colon and colon are always placed outside the quotation marks.

VIII. *Bible Versions*

    A. Versions of the Bible quoted must be specified in the text of the manuscript (as AV, RSV, Moffatt, Goodspeed, Phillips, etc.).

    B. *All quotations from Scripture must be carefully checked for accuracy by the author*. It has been our experience that passages quoted from memory are rarely accurate.

IX. *Permissions to Quote*

    A. Wherever and whenever the author quotes, word for word, any material copyrighted in another book, magazine, etc., it is his responsibility to secure *written* permission from the original copyright source. Quoted material may include tables, charts and illustrations, as well as extracts from the text.

    B. Some publishers have a form which they forward to authors who request permission to quote from their books; such forms require the following general information:

        1. Title and author of book from which quotation is desired.

        2. Nature of the work for which the selection is desired.

        3. Your name as author or compiler requesting permission.

        4. Name of publisher by whom your book is to be published.

        5. Intended time of publication.

        6. Selections desired. (These are to be specifically designated by giving the first word of the quotation and the page on which it appears and the last word and the page on which it appears.)

        7. Total pages or total lines to be quoted.

C. It is not necessary to obtain permission to quote from books out of copyright.

D. While there is no hard and fast rule as to how many words a quotation may contain and not require permission, we ask that such permission be secured in writing wherever the quotation is of *fifty* or more words.

E. In the matter of quoting poetry, permission must be secured for using as little as two lines, because of the highly concentrated nature of the material. There is usually a fee, payable by the author, involved in such permission.

F. Be sure to include the name of the book, author, publisher, copyright date and page reference in all permission statements. We prefer the following forms for acknowledgments:

1. For quoting from a book: Melvin E. Wheatley, Jr., *Going His Way* (Westwood, N.J., Fleming H. Revell Company, 1957), p. 10.

2. For quoting from a periodical: B. H. Lane, "A Uniform Scheme for Citations," *Science,* Vol. 75 (April 10), pp. 390-392.

3. For quoting poetry: Mary Dixon Thayer, "A Prayer," from *Sonnets* (New York, The Macmillan Company, 1933).

G. The proper placing in the book of credit lines, permissions and acknowledgments will be left to the discretion of the publisher.

X. *Copyrights*

A. The copyright for your book will be secured by your publisher. This copyright holds for a period of twenty-eight years, when it may be renewed (only once) for a second twenty-eight-year period, after which the copyright expires.

B. Titles of books cannot be copyrighted.

XI. *Shipping*

A. Pages of your manuscript should be separate—not fastened together in any way—and the manuscript should be mailed or expressed flat, not rolled.

B. Return postage must be enclosed unless otherwise specified by the publisher; otherwise manuscripts are returned to the author, if unacceptable, by mail or express collect.

Read Section IX carefully; in the business of quoting and permissions to quote lie deadly pitfalls for the careless author. Publishers take permissions seriously; many of them have people reading the books of other publishers for unacknowledged quotations. Your manuscript will get the same attention that your income tax report gets in the Bureau of Internal Revenue, and heaven help you when you slip! Failure to acknowledge or secure permission can and often does result in demand for payment or a lawsuit; worse than that, it can label an author at the beginning of his career as one who borrows with too heavy a hand. And watch those quotations from Scripture. Publishers of new versions of the Bible, such as the Revised Standard Version, hold copyrights on their books, and they have very definite requirements in the matter of quotations from their texts. Be on the safe side, and write the publishers of those versions about it, no matter how many words are involved. Then you are not only safe legally; you are doing the courteous thing.

When you quote Scripture, quote it with the original source at your side, and check it. Believe it or not, preachers are notorious for inaccuracy and carelessness in quoting Holy Writ; they garble, misspell, misquote, mix various versions, give credit to Matthew when they should give it to Luke or give no reference at all. Some just write their own version, in order to make it say what they want it to say. Days and even weeks of a copy editor's time are often consumed in a maddening and often fruitless search to verify quotations that are all out of line, or in correcting it once it has been found. Cite it right, check and double-check, *and let the poor editor know from which version you are quoting.*

Never hand the publisher or editor a pep talk before you send in your manuscript; they pay no attention to letters from famous acquaintances of the author, informing him that you, John Doe, are an up-and-coming author and that you have a masterpiece that will stop literary traffic. The publisher will decide whether or not you are up-and-coming, at least so far as he is concerned.

Send it to one publisher at a time. Some hopeful neophytes mimeograph their masterpieces and send them to a dozen editors at once, in the same mail. The minute an editor senses that, you're done. Editors and publishers do not like to be put in competition against each other by the author. It is also ethically wrong to put one publisher to the trouble and expense of record keeping, editorial reading, possible outside editorial reading, etc., only to discover when he offers to accept your manuscript that it has already been accepted by another! This editors and publishers will not tolerate. Do you blame them?

Send it to a reliable, established house. Study the catalogue of the house before you send it. Some houses publish books in the liberal field, some in the conservative. Some are denominational, some independent. Don't send a manuscript defending infant baptism to a Baptist house, or one condemning Arminianism to the Methodists. Beware of the "vanity" publisher who demands payment from you for publishing your book. He doesn't publish it; he merely prints it, on a cost-plus basis; he will give you little or no advertising or promotion. You are in for trouble—financial and otherwise—when you try that. If your work is worth publishing, it should be able to stand on its own legs, and pay its own way.

If and when your manuscript is accepted, *let the editors and the publishers alone.* Give them credit for knowing how to edit, print, bind and circulate your book. They know more about paper and type than you do; they know what will impress the customer and what will offend him, what will make him want to buy your book and what will make him put it down and walk away.

Read the contract the publisher sends you. Read the small

print. Be sure you know what you are getting, what is expected of the publisher and what he expects of you. Read especially such clauses as these, found in all standard contracts, in one form or another:

"The Author agrees to deliver to the Publisher a complete typewritten [editors never read longhand manuscripts] manuscript of the work in final form *satisfactory to the Publisher.*" If it is not satisfactory, the publisher can refuse to publish, other contractural arrangements notwithstanding.

"If . . . retyping is necessary, the Publisher shall have the right to edit and retype the manuscript *and charge the cost to the Author.*"

"The cost of alterations in proof [the first printed form of your book] required by the Author, other than corrections of printer's errors, shall be compared with the original cost of composition and any amount in excess of 10 per cent of the original cost of composition shall be charged against any payments due the Author under this Agreement." [The first book this author wrote cost him $200 for elaborate and unnecessary corrections he made in proof, which he should have made in the manuscript. He never did *that* again!]

"The Publisher shall pay to the Author . . . 10 per cent of the retail price of the book." Ten per cent is standard. Yes, you can demand more royalty, and you might even get it, but the "more" will come out of advertising and/or promotion allowances. Jumping the royalty usually means putting a higher price on the book—which means fewer sales. You are far better off with 10 per cent and good advertising and promotion than you are with 12½ per cent with limited advertising and promotion. The publisher, after all his costs are paid, seldom makes anywhere near 10 per cent on his investment—and he invests anywhere from five to ten thousand dollars in your book—and up. If he makes from 3 to 5 per cent, he is happy about the whole thing. Don't be unreasonable with him; he has all the headaches.

"On copies of any edition bound in paper or other less expensive binding (the publisher) pays 5 per cent of the retail price in royalty." This is because these books are sold at a lower price, and the difference in the cost of a hard binding and a paper binding is not sufficient to justify this lower price without, also, a lower royalty.

Check the items dealing with book club editions, with lease of plates to other publishers, with sheets or duplicate plates sold for export. No royalties are paid on copies of your book given away for review or promotion, or on copies damaged by fire or water, or on copies sold as "remainders," or below cost.

Memorize the "option clause": "In consideration of this Agreement, the Author agrees to make his first offer of his next work to the Publisher on terms to be arranged." That is only fair, and it is included in all contracts. The publisher has taken all the financial risks involved in your first book, and if you do well with it, it would seem that he is entitled to a chance to publish your second one. Only in rare cases is this clause deleted.

Some authors like to "shop around," from one publisher to another. This is dangerous. Get a good publisher and stay with him. When a publisher discovers that an author has published with a dozen different houses, he is immediately suspicious; it can mean that a lot of manuscripts have been rejected by eleven out of the twelve, or that the author is hard to live with. The best guarantee of the success of a book lies in the cooperation of editor and writer over a long period of years. Thomas Wolfe and the famed Maxwell Perkins (editor for Scribner's) were a perfect team, producing Wolfe's finest books. When Wolfe left Perkins, his work began to decline.

Above all, be not discouraged when the manuscript is declined. There has never been an author without rejection slips. It is part of your learning how. A rejection tests the mettle of the author; if he quits, he just "ain't got it in here," as Archy, laying his hand over his heart, said to Mehitabel in one of Don Marquis' beautiful books. If he is worth his salt, he will profit by rejection. Joshua Liebman's *Peace of Mind* was rejected many times before it saw the light of day; Robert Louis Stevenson had the time of his life getting his first book published; *David Harum* wasn't published until after its author was dead.

Write, write, write, however the acceptances or rejections fall. If you have it, you'll get there. It is a hard, long road—as long and as hard as great preaching—and quite as fruitful and rewarding. Write, write, write!

4

Public Relations in Your Community

JAMES L. CHRISTENSEN

ONCE IN A while every Christian minister feels isolated. He may feel that he is out of touch with the realities of life, or that he is not making any impact upon the inner life of his community. He wants to multiply his influence to the utmost, but his congregation seems to make but small impact. He becomes impatient with the slow progress of Christian maturity and disillusioned by the prevailing and entrenched conditions in areas of his city. Brooding over his circumstance, he flees to the desert for refuge and comfort. It may be the spiritual desert of his own heart. Likely it is the social desert of his own congregation. There he broods.

Many ministers of Christ, whether they recognize it or not, are perpetually on the edge of a social and spiritual desert. They conduct services and preach sermons. They visit sick people and attend gatherings within their own congregation. But the scope of their work and influence, as of their thought, is limited. They actually live and work as if their very faith had separated them from the common life of their community.

No greater fallacy could haunt a minister of Jesus Christ. There is literally no other profession which gives such a wide opportunity for influence. There is no other molder of opinion to which human minds are more accessible. The businessman's life is cramped. The lawyer's life moves in a groove. The journalist all too often meets people on the surface. The minister, if he is alert, is set in the midst of tremendous possibilities.

COOPERATION IN THE COMMUNITY

Two pictures illustrate diverse attitudes demonstrated by ministers.

The first picture is of two mules that are tied together by a rope around their necks. Each stands near a stack of hay, but not near enough to eat. The picture shows the mules straining with all their might, each pulling toward his own haystack, but with no result except that each is finding it harder and harder to breathe. That is competition.

In the second picture, both mules are peacefully eating at one haystack, and in the final scene they have moved to the other haystack. That is cooperation.

Today we are living in a social climate that demands less independence and more interdependence. It is the conviction of this writer that the minister should be leading the way to cooperative living and to brotherhood through Jesus Christ.

The temptation for the minister is to go his separate way with his separate program, indifferent to others in the community.

The minister who realizes that he is a part of the team, however, and makes every effort to cooperate, will be respected and his influence will be broadened.

With Other Ministers and Churches

Cooperation should start with members of one's own profession. Someone has observed that people are generally jealous only of persons engaged in the same kind of business. Bankers are envious of other bankers, teachers are jealous of other teachers, doctors compete with other doctors. Ministers are never jealous—except of other ministers!

Some pastors find it impossible to associate, much less work, with those of another denomination or faith. This is extremely unfortunate, for it leaves division and alienation in the Christian community and witness.

Though there may be differences of theology, practice, and

opinion, yet there is a broad base of agreement. To that extent, and without compromising convictions, it is possible for the minister to cooperate with other ministers of the Christian faith. The interpenetration of personalities and ideas is personally rewarding. Even more significant, by working together some things can be accomplished in a community that separately cannot be. The facts of our world's chaos and sin should bind all clergymen together into a fraternal relationship. The minister who is too busy to associate himself with his brethren in the ministerial association or to attend conferences and conventions is circumventing his influence.

The minister of a cooperative spirit will write a note of welcome to a new minister in the city, drop by his study to meet him, give him a city map, offer assistance, and invite him to the next ministerial meeting. When interdenominational groups meet, they depend upon the leadership of those who show consistent, genuine interest. When the minister's denominational conventions meet he should rearrange his schedule to include them.

A conscientious minister will consciously cultivate good rapport and engender good will by writing congratulations to a fellow minister who has written a book, received a degree, rendered an outstanding service, presented a commendable radio program, or been honored.

Though the chasm separating the Protestant clergyman from the Roman Catholic priest or the Jewish rabbi is great, even so there is sufficient common ground in the monotheistic faith and heritage to warrant congenial fellowship and some cooperation.

With the Healing Team

The minister needs likewise to be cooperative as a part of the healing team. The physician, psychologist, psychiatrist and psychotherapist have their distinct roles. Nonetheless, the minister is a vital part of the treatment team, also. He can render his contribution without trespassing upon the other's domain.

However, he must always realize his limitations and work in co-operation with others on the team.

The task of the religious leader is to be a spiritual adviser. He is the physician to the wounded in soul. In this day of science, the minister is tempted to try to be a psychiatrist or to use the methods of the psychologist, or to think of himself as a therapist or a social caseworker. An understanding of these fields is an invaluable aid; nevertheless, he must not abdicate his peculiar, symbolic role as moral and spiritual leader. The distinctive role of the pastor needs clarification and appreciation by other members of the healing team as well. Hence, close cooperation is necessary on the part of all.

The minister would do well, therefore, to acquaint himself by a personal visit with the hospital administrators, the psychologists and psychiatrists, as many physicians as possible, and the many community resources available to meet people's problems. Such a visit need not be lengthy, just long enough to make himself known and to assure them of his desire to cooperate in every way possible in mutual service. Such an overture in itself leaves the impression that he is informed and has the proper spirit.

When visiting the sick, the minister should remember that the physician or psychiatrist is in full charge of the patient. The minister assumes, therefore, a subordinate, supporting ministry of cooperation. To the patient, he will always build up confidence and faith in the doctor. Never will he speak critically, nor discredit a physician regardless of his personal opinion or knowledge of weaknesses or failures. When the minister says, "You have such a capable and skillful physician," it will help allay the hidden fears of the patient. Under no circumstance will the minister prescribe or diagnose for a patient. To do so is a serious breach of ethics. In regard to emotionally disturbed mental patients, extreme conscientiousness must be exercised. It will be well for the clergyman to visit personally with the attending doctor to demonstrate cooperation and to ask for his advice on what he may suggest from the pastor.

The pastor should visit the sick in hospital and home with regularity and as frequently as the seriousness demands. It is never advisable to linger long in the sickroom. Always the minister should be cheerful, yet dignified and quiet. News of other sick patients should not be discussed.

Whether to pray for the sick is a decision which the minister must "play by ear." If the patient is a fine Christian accustomed to praying, he may ask the pastor to pray, thus to sustain his faith. Prayer may be unadvisable if it will unnerve the patient, create fear, or is an unaccustomed practice, for the patient may conclude that he is near "death's door," and that this is a desperate, emergency procedure. If such spiritual exercises cause embarrassment, it may be best to refrain from vocal prayer, or to write out a prayer and leave it with the patient and family.

The pastor, on occasions, will need to make referrals to the psychiatrist or phychologist. A prerequisite for close cooperation in this field is an understanding on the part of the minister of the symptoms of mental illness. The minister is in a unique position because danger signals can be detected early and referrals made before permanent irreparable damage is done.

With Social Agencies

The church and the social agencies are rediscovering that they have common roots and common motivation in serving needy people, hence are in need of one another. The minister is ethically committed to refer a person in need to the persons or agencies that can best meet his problem.

Most every community has social services and resources which are not in competition to the pastor's work, but which complement his ministry. The minister may not have the time, technique, or proper channel to meet the needs of some people. Therefore, he needs to know the resources available in his own community. He might ask himself the questions: "Where do I go if a man wants a job? Where do I go if a transient wants a meal and a room for the night? Where do I go for help with an alcoholic? Where do I go when parents wonder if their child is retarded? Where do I go if a husband and wife are having difficulty and it seems to be a deeper problem than I feel adequate to handle? Where do I go if a family does not have sufficient clothing to send a child to school? Where do I go if there is an older person who needs nursing-home care but does not have the funds to provide it? Where do I go if a boy wants to study for the ministry but is not sure whether or not he has the intellectual capacity to finish college? Where do I go to find help or a foster home for a neglected child? Where do I go to find help for a family that needs legal assistance but cannot afford to hire an attorney? How do I find out if a person or family has been consulting other agencies?" Charles F. Kemp's handy workbook, "The Pastor and Community Resources" is an invaluable aid to the minister in this regard. Important guidance is given in the listing of the different social agencies to which referrals can be made.

The pastor could beneficially spend time in getting acquainted with the men and women who work in the employment bureau, family service association, community welfare council, child guidance clinics, Alcoholics Anonymous, nursing homes, police department, Red Cross, Salvation Army, and so forth.

The pastor's role in cooperation is to recognize the need, to provide information so people know what the possibilities are, to create the atmosphere by which such help will be desired and accepted, and to interpret the general procedures for approaching the agency. After finding a specialized resource for a needy person, the pastor's responsibility is not over. He still should maintain an active interest in said person and seek to continue a pastoral ministry.

The pastor can do much to foster cooperation by serving on boards and committees of such agencies and by encouraging his people to do so.

With the Funeral Directors

It is desirable that the minister and funeral directors work in close cooperation. When one first enters a parish he should become acquainted with the reputable morticians. At such a time, it would be well to inquire regarding community custom. Though one is not necessarily bound by the traditions of the past, yet it perhaps is unwise to assume the role of an unorthodox revolutionary who insists upon doing everything his own way.

In some communities the eulogy is customarily a part of the funeral service. However much one dislikes this anachronism, and there are sufficient reasons for eliminating it, yet it is best to cooperate with tradition until by gradual training the custom can be changed.

Nowhere in the funeral service is there more need for reform than in the music. Many communities are coming more and more to organ music only, thus eliminating the troublesome problem of emotion-packed, "tear-jerking" favorite hymns that tend to undo all the solace that the minister strives to sustain. Wherein this custom prevails, however, it seems best to express to the funeral directors your personal wishes, to seek to train your congregation in the selection of appropriate music, and to counsel with the bereaved before the selections are made.

The modern funeral, to be sure, is greatly secularized with overemphasis upon the streamlined design of caskets, protective vaults, lifelike make-up for the corpse, and sprays of flowers as if there were security in these. The minister's initial reaction is disgust and the inclination to criticize the directors for parading their funeral wares.

Prudence, however, dictates that the minister use the time at his disposal to lift up the spiritual qualities of life and death, to depreciate the physical, and to bring spiritual comfort to the bereft. Through his church he can introduce the "memorial fund" procedure for a lasting memento rather than flowers, which are so temporary. In a growing friendship with the directors and members of his own congregation, he can counsel the wisdom of keeping the casket closed.

"He preached forty-five minutes," was the recent disrespectful remark of a funeral director regarding an inconsiderate, thoughtless minister's funeral service. He had a right to complain. The funeral service is not an occasion for lengthy exposition, eulogy, or preaching. Seldom should a service be longer than twenty minutes, and should consist of soul-inspiring, faith-building Scripture, prayers and meditation, accompanied by quieting music. Brevity will be appreciated by the family, friends, and all concerned, and will build a reputation of good judgment for the minister.

The scheduling of the funeral service can be an area of misunderstanding, therefore the pastor should counsel with the funeral directors involved to understand the procedure. Generally, it is basic courtesy for the director to consult the pastor to learn when he is available before determining the time. It must be mutually understood by all concerned that the pastor is busy with many appointments, some of which cannot be juggled, the funeral director may have several services to schedule, and the family may have its own peculiar circumstances which are paramount in consideration. On rare occasions, services have been announced in the newspaper for a certain time, even before the presiding clergyman had been notified. This is inexcusable. When mutual time schedules are difficult, the pastor should endeavor to adjust his schedule to that which best serves the family and director's advantage. This will evidence a spirit of cooperation and will be deeply appreciated.

With the Public School System

Protestantism has a great stake in the public school system in America.

Frequently, ministers are inclined to voice their protests at the discipline, actions, and secularization of the public school. To be sure these are rightful concerns; nonetheless, if the alternative to public schools is a competitive parochial system, then Protestantism could easily be absorbed by the well-organized, traditional Roman Catholic system. Too, a competitive parochial system would only more sharply define the religious barriers which are already too apparent in many communities.

Without infringement upon the separation of church and state, it is possible for the fair-minded, conscientious minister to cooperate in many ways to demonstrate his interest in public education. He is an educated man himself and certainly should have a legitimate interest in school affairs.

It would be well for a minister to attend an occasional meeting of the school board, for no other reason than to indicate his interest. He needs to learn firsthand the quality of the local school system. He should become acquainted with the superintendent of schools, the administrative officials, and the school board members. If he has children in the public schools, he should assume at least a normal amount of interest in the school where his own children attend. He might visit the classroom, or an occasional assembly, or offer to share impressions of a trip with the class. When asked to hold membership in or speak at P.T.A. metings, he should accept graciously. The children and youth from his church will be elated if their minister shows interest in their affairs.

Frequently, having his children's teachers as dinner guests in the home is a rewarding experience. Amid informal, congenial surroundings mutual understanding is more readily possible.

The wise minister will never take unfair advantage of the school system by attempting to use it for sectarian advantages.

UTILIZING COMMUNITY ORGANIZATIONS

The Christian minister living in the world seeks to accomplish God's will through membership in many groups, including his family, his church, his community fellowship, and his political allegiance. Some organizations in a community may come into competition with the church. However, there are many that are legitimate parallel organizations, seeking goals which strengthen the work of the church.

Every force that ennobles and lifts the lives of people deserves the minister's cooperation and moral support. Actually, the pastor should participate in many community-betterment programs because he is a responsible citizen, and should maintain friendly relations with leaders in all areas of civic improvement. Frequently, pastors have become outstanding leaders in various cultural and character-building clubs or humanitarian enterprises in their cities. They have been the motivators of unselfish ideals and broadened sympathies. Here is a field lying beyond that of worship and pastoral care in which the minister can make his service count effectively.

However, even the most enthusiastic joiner cannot and should not affiliate with every one of the numerous social interest groups so characteristic of our culture. The endless number of such groups can dissipate the energies, time and resources of a popular minister until he has no strength for service to his own flock. The church must remain first in the pastor's heart. It is not always necessary for him to become a joiner of everything or to work directly with agencies to be an influential community leader. His greatest contribution may be giving his congregation the motivation, direction and encouragement to serve the larger life of the city.

Nonetheless, there is a legitimate place for a minister in some of the community organizations which afford him an unparalleled opportunity for broadening the influence of his ministry. A minister should never want his church to be insulated from all contact with community life.

There is a need, then, for astute ministerial leadership so that the church can utilize these organizations in so far as they provide resources for achieving Christian goals, or can oppose these organizations in so far as they provide resistance to the realization of the Christian hope.

Standard for Assessing

A minister must be careful in the choice of the organizations to which he belongs. In judging the worthiness of an organization, it is confusing to resort to a literal rendering of the Bible because its authority has been used to support almost every kind of enterprise—even sub-Christian ones. The pluralism of the churches demonstrates a wide diversity of opinion varying with geographic, economic or cultural conditions. The individual's conscience is far from infallible, for its content depends upon its previous insight and experience.

There is no exact way of establishing that any organized movement is absolutely good or absolutely evil. Standards for judgment must be provided by the sources of Christian perspective as seen in the dimensions of the gospel. He should not just ask, "Is this good?" or "Is this good for something?" Rather, the minister should ask, "Is this good for furthering the will of God?" "Does this organization minister to the real needs of the persons involved? Does it give a chance to fulfill potentialities for good in the service of God? Does it make one a better person in all his relationships with others?"

An organization cannot be tested chiefly in terms of developing the qualities of its particular members, but in terms of whether it concerns itself with the good for everyone. If a service club embraces the fellowship of its members at the cost of being oblivious to the real needs of others in the vicinity, it has thereby limited its field of usefulness. Insofar as the organization fulfills these requirements, it may be a resource for the achieving of the Christian hope; insofar as it is in conflict with the ideal of "loving your neighbor as yourself," and "do unto others as you would that they do unto you," it is in resistance to the Christian goal.

As ministers, we are concerned that the social order shall be sufficiently Christian to provide freedom, social fellowship, and opportunity for service for every man. Can the organization in question contribute anything that is good to the social order?

Does the organization's work achieve a respect for personality?
Does the club concern itself with the needs of the community? Does it alleviate suffering on a world-wide scale? Are the
attitudes expressed in conflict with the church? Are the projects
and activities indifferent to the spirit of Jesus Christ?

Fraternal and Service Groups

Should the minister belong to a service club or fraternal
order? There are three possible attitudes. One extreme is for
the Christian minister to denounce fraternalism as an unfair
competitor to the church, and to make every effort at resistance
to it. Organized fraternalism (in which is included lodges, service clubs, veterans' auxiliaries, women's groups and country
clubs) does compete with the church for the time, interest,
loyalty, and resources of its members. Too, fraternalism with its
reckless use of quasi-religious and pseudo-Biblical language
often impairs a proper understanding of true religious experience, and is often accepted as a religious substitute. Fraternal
organizations are fundamentally exclusive and often confirm
the attitude and injustices which the church is committed to
resist. Hence, some ministers insist that no member of the
church can remain in good standing and be involved in any
fraternal life. The result is most unfortunate. The church de-
prives itself of every potential gain that might come from contact with this significant part of modern civic life and of becoming a leavening influence within such.

The other extreme for the minister is to take fraternalism
at its own exaggerated self-evaluation, treating it as though it
were a genuinely religious institution, on a par with the church.
Some ministers, for example, throw themselves into fraternal
life without restraint, giving the impression that they regard it
as being practically equivalent with the church.

The third approach for the minister is to look at fraternalism
as it really is, limited, inadequate, secular; yet at the same time
to see the potential resources for the church. The fellowship,

spirit of service, world-wide interest and above-average standard of conduct of fraternal groups are inherent opportunities by which the fraternal club can become an ally of the minister and church.

To be sure, banal, often vulgar, and adolescent habits are typical of many service clubs. However, the friendly, relaxed, informal spirit provides an opportunity for the minister to develop mutual appreciation and understanding of community men in ways not often possible in the more reserved contacts of ordinary, casual relationships. The attitude of concern of one another's welfare which is an integral part of lodge life is wholesome, though it may fall short of the aim of real brotherhood.

The ideal of service for which the church aims goes far beyond the service club attempts, yet through the fraternal groups members do learn the satisfactions that come from giving practical help to others. The undertakings of the clubs usually are immediately at hand, personally appealing, and easily visualized, and provide training in unselfishness. This is a great resource for the church in harnessing service to the tasks of Christian brotherhood. The minister has a tremendous opportunity to inculcate the gospel.

Most service clubs and fraternal groups, likewise, are worldwide in scope, and have a definite goal of promoting international understanding and good will. A minister can help the club to make much of this purpose, and can creatively and energetically keep it before the club. The highest officials of these clubs are vitally interested in this phase, which opens the door for presentation of the Christian ideal of world brotherhood. One may protest that the incentive came in the first place from the church and should be kept there. Nonetheless, a realistic approach is that the international interest of the fraternal groups is a positive asset to the church in building world community. Wisely used, the minister can use this leverage to combat within the fraternity itself the exclusive, snobbish, race-conscious, reactionary attitudes which are resistant factors.

Having said this, however, the minister's cooperation must have limitations. The minister must never cease to be discriminating in his evaluation of fraternal groups. His own integrity demands that he shall never approve nor condone those aspects in fraternal life which conflict with Christian aims or standards. This requires constant vigilance and possible misunderstandings and friction. However, where a minister can do so, without compromise of his own convictions, he can further the Christian cause in his community.

The decision to be a member of a fraternal group may depend upon the size of the community in which he serves. The smaller the community, the more impressive and influential the fraternal groups in community life. The importance of such organizations appears to be in inverse ratio to the size of the city. The same thing is true of the churches, which means that the church and club in the smaller town will have many of the same members. If many of the minister's constituents are members of a club, he may wish to belong where his influence will be greater. If he is in a large metropolitan city where none of his members belong and where the club is mainly fellowship, he may wish not to belong.

Social and Welfare Agencies

Should the minister give time and leadership to community social and welfare agencies? Again opinions differ, with some amount of justification.

There is no small amount of resentment on the part of some clergymen who feel that the so-called "secular" agencies have invaded what they consider to be the province of the church, hence have displaced much of the church's charitable and benevolent work. Hence, these agencies are considered competitive to the church for men's time, talent, and money, and tend to blunt the idealism and demand for social justice. It is an understandable reaction, for at one time, to be sure, the church did heal the sick, provide for the poor, educate and train the young, and care for the aged and homeless.

If the church had been doing a satisfactory job in "binding up the wounds and setting captives free," however, men would not have welcomed another liberator, nor given their money to other organized philanthropy or social work. Fundamentally, the church is at fault because of its own meager efforts.

Actually, the Christian spirit has been infused into much secular work (for most social service historically has rooted in the Christian heritage) until there seems to be very little difference between the better enterprises under secular auspices and the better work supported by religious groups. The quantity of work done by the church is not adequate to the demands of today's expanding, complex society.

Therefore, it would seem advisable for a minister to support the distinctive church work, and also to give leadership to the community social agencies, because both should be serving the purposes of God in contemporary life.

A minister has unlimited opportunities and is needed in organized philanthropic work to keep alive the religious values, to give affirmative religious insights to help proceed on the basis of religious assumptions, to help select Christian personnel with a high sense of vocation, and to give expression to the way and purposes of *agape*.

The "philanthropic foundation" is one of the major businesses in America today, and each year the social welfare state is emerging with alarming pace. Mammoth agencies are now existent to serve lesser agencies. All of this confuses the scene.

Four danger areas in which the minister can help the social agency are:

First, the minister can ask the welfare and service agencies to help people in such a way that they will help themselves, to create a concern on the part of the recipients for other's welfare, and to witness to the "source from whom all blessings flow" and whose spirit motivates unselfish concern. Social work must be more than "doing good to people"; it should have the quality for transforming character if it is to be a religious resource.

Second, the minister can insist not only that physical assistance be available, but that qualities of the spirit and human kindness be introduced as well, that "impersonal professionalism" give way to genuine personal interest in individuals.

Third, constant re-examination of the purposes of the agencies is needed so that they do not come into conflict with the established programs of the church or other agencies, or so the institution does not become an end in itself or does not vie for prestige and publicity for itself at the expense of others.

Evaluation of cooperating agencies and those hopefully anticipating getting into the "chest" is a generally accepted policy in most cities. However, there appears to be very little long-range, over-all, broad planning. Too, unpopular causes or agencies are sometimes discriminated against. Rivalry between agencies sometimes occurs when apportionment of Community Chest funds are made.

Herein the minister can exert a spiritual undergirding that will retain magnanimity, cooperation, and fairness.

Community Politics

Should a minister take part in politics? Frequently one hears the admonition, "Preach the gospel. Stay out of politics!"

True, the minister should refrain from any public involvement in partisan politics. It is not uncommon to learn of a minister being a candidate for political office, or one giving political advice from the pulpit, thus revealing his political leanings. Such happenings are unfortunate and usually out of place.

The separation of the institutions of church and state does not mean that politics and religion are to be divorced. The gospel certainly does have social and political implications and applications. It should be the minister's interest to speak to the conscience of the city or nation regarding political issues; yet, it should be done kindly, without partisanship. A minister is the prophet of God constantly submitting the political behavior of our nation to the judgment of God. It is the minister's duty as a citizen to be informed in the democratic procedure of government, and to keep Americans aware of the spiritual roots from whence it has flowed.

General Omar Bradley declared that ministers have done more for sustaining democracy than any other group of people. The Christian minister can become a most sought-after speaker, hence broaden his influence, by speaking up for American democracy at its best and warning citizens of the threats. If he is a student of communism and can evaluate objectively the current struggle, he should do so. He will not speak as though Christianity and democracy were synonymous. He will not act as if democracy were utopia. He will not assume that the survival of Christianity depends upon democracy. Nonetheless, he will speak of the qualities that have made America a great nation, of the American dream of freedom under God for all men, of the spiritual roots which keep democracy alive, and of the responsibilities of freedom.

The clergyman is expected to be a good citizen himself, registering as a voter and urging his congregation to do likewise. One well-known church sets up a registration booth, and at the proper season urges Christians to register and vote. Naturally, the minister and his family will vote and urge the congregation to do likewise. The pastor never tells his constituents for *whom* to vote. It is possible, however, to urge investigation by voters of the candidates' moral and spiritual commitments. The minister should never publicly endorse one particular political candidate.

When moral issues are at stake, the minister, as a spokesman for God, should make a stand and lift his voice against legislation that threatens to harm humanity, and for legislation that benefits man's spiritual, mental, or physical needs. Many such issues will be controversial in nature. The minister's approach and spirit are all important. He will need to be able to see both sides of issues, to withhold judgment until facts are apparent, to be independent of pressure groups, to love all the individuals involved, and to speak kindly, yet persuasively, what he interprets to be God's will.

What absorbs a minister reveals the quality, maturity, and

understanding of his Christian commitment. Many times the typical minister makes quite a "noise" over relatively inconsequential issues, and remains strangely silent on the rightful major concerns. He may be absorbed with his trivial "pet peeves" until he gives little time or energy to the major challenges. It takes saintly sanity and Christian statesmanship to know where and of what to take hold.

It is well for a minister to attend city council meetings occasionally to bear witness to his interest in municipal affairs. This will also increase his stature in the minds of the commissioners. When matters pertaining to the moral welfare of the city are discussed, he should be there so that the spiritual forces have a voice. When the city government does something for the community, he should be generous in writing letters of commendation. Chamber of commerce secretaries and mayors must feel that ministers are born in the "objective case" because about the only time they hear from them is when they "object." The more positive, complimentary, constructive approach will make the minister's influence greater, his judgments more respected; then, his criticisms, when given, will be listened to with seriousness.

Radical Causes

Opinions differ and will continue to differ as to how far it is advisable for the minister to align himself with specific radical causes. It is impossible to lay down any general rule applicable to all cases. Individual participation carries with it institutional participation, if not officially or legally, then practically. Involvements have brought sad, disillusioning experiences for many.

Radical groups have as their objective concern causes with which a minister usually can heartily agree to some degree— better working conditions for laborers, improved wages, control of liquor trade, or some other "pet interests."

A minister should be aware of high-sounding political pressure groups which may be masquerading under the guise of Christianity. Some organizations are actively opposed to the church and Christian idealism. They try to use the ministers while plotting to minimize the church's influence. To these the minister must be unutterably opposed. He needs to know enough not to get burned by "communistic front" or super-charged patriotic groups.

ALERT TO UNUSUAL OPPORTUNITIES

Why is it some ministers are catapulted into the public eye, while others equally talented are not? Apparently, some have no more ability than their colleagues, yet they reach a wider audience and their influence is more deeply felt.

One reason, perhaps, is that some ministers are more alert to timely opportunities. All great men are products of their times. It is not always "what they have known" or "whom they know," but where they have been, how they have handled situations, and how alert they were to opportunities. The wise molders of public opinion have had the courage to speak at the proper moment, and the wisdom to remain discreetly silent at other times. They have been able to see opportunities in calamities, to sense the needs in chaotic times, to discern necessary reforms needed in communities, and the creativity to meet the dramatic moments of a community's life with a witness for God.

Timely Issues

The press is quick to pick up statements from a level-headed, objective minister regarding issues of community interest. James Pike, the controversial Episcopal bishop, was put in the national spotlight by countering Cardinal Spellman's recommended censorship of the movie "Baby Doll," by criticizing the Roman hierarchy's resistance to artificial birth control, and by writing, for example, on "Should There Be a Roman Catholic in the White House?" Bishop Pike is alert to timely issues, and feels sufficiently informed to express and defend his opinions.

Dr. W. A. Criswell, minister of the First Baptist Church in Dallas, Texas, took advantage of the battle within the Texas legislature in 1959 to dismiss all atheists from the faculty of Texas University, by preaching a lengthy series of sermons on "Evolution and Christianity." This had front-page news coverage across the state for weeks.

The discerning minister will be alert to the issues about which people are troubled, and cause them to look to the church for help. It will require factual research, objectivity, maturity of judgment, and a clear articulation to "walk where angels fear to tread."

Many opportunities for communication are open to the enterprising minister. The most obvious, of course, is the sermon medium. There are public relations values in the timely, catchy sermon topics advertised in the local community press, parish paper, and outdoor bulletin. Letters of invitation to community citizens especially interested in the topic discussed will be appreciated.

The panel discussion at a civic club, P.T.A., or church meeting affords the minister an opportunity to either participate (if asked) or to ask pertinent questions. I personally have found such experiences very rewarding and helpful in my witness as a minister. Among the panel discussions which have seemed most beneficial have been those dealing with: Our National Purpose, Discipline of Youth, Capital Punishment, Mental Health, Juvenile Delinquency, Community Problems, Politics and the Christians, and Church Family Life.

One minister has a "Summer Forum" on Sunday evenings in which a variety of timely issues are discussed to a large, appreciative, public-minded congregation. He has had such programs as a review of Dr. Zhivago and other timely books, a debate of a current issue, and a symposium on the National Council of Churches.

The "Letters to the Editor" column of the local paper and

the magazines of larger circulation is an excellent medium for ministers to present their views. One should not write too frequently, nor dogmatically, as if he were a "ministerial crank or fanatic." Clear, concise, logical, brief letters carry the most weight.

Community Visitors

Every community at one time or another has the fortune of welcoming a well-known visitor. He may be the President of the United States, a famous author, a movie star, athlete, opera singer, a great churchman, or a foreign visitor. The alert minister can capitalize upon such occasions. Care should be taken to make sure the visitor is a Christian example, if the church would use him to advantage rather than detriment.

The Christian Athletes Association was organized for the very purpose of witnessing for Christ through famous athletes. Alvin Dark, Bobby Morrow, Bud Wilkinson, and Bob Richards, to mention only a few, have been used in this athletic-minded age to witness for Christ.

When a churchman of wide reputation visits in the community or adjacent area, an alert minister many times can arrange an interview or speaking engagement. After securing permission of the sponsoring party, he may write in advance to see if a speaking engagement is possible. If not, then at least a TV interview or press interview will prove helpful. Dr. Frank Laubach, Paul Tillich, Dan Poling, Norman Vincent Peale, Ralph Sockman are frequent travelers across America and names with tremendous public relations value.

Perhaps more difficult to arrange, and requiring more discrimination, is the movie star. Those such as Roy Rogers, Dale Evans, and Pat Boone have been most generous with their time and have a powerful testimony for the Lord to give to youth.

One of my most broadening experiences was serving as chairman of the foreign visitors committee of our local chamber of commerce. In this position I met and arranged the speaking

agenda of each foreign visitor, and many times introduced them
to the various audiences, which took in nearly every segment of
our community in a year's time.

Community Needs

Dr. Harry Emerson Fosdick closes his autobiography with a
chapter entitled "Ideas That Have Used Me." He became an
influential religious leader not only because of his speaking and
writing ability, but because of the issues which he championed.

Today every community has causes and voices clamoring for
the minister's time, energy, and influence. He must choose carefully the "ideas that he would allow to use him," for we are all
used by some.

I am thinking of a ministerial colleague of mine who is a
tremendous community influence because he has sensed some
of the community problems affecting youth. He has allowed
himself to be "used by" a youth development board studying
such problems as the periodic outburts of warfare between our
servicemen and the local teen-agers, the narcotic smuggling
among youth, pornographic literature and Hallowe'en vandal-
ism. This study focused the community's attention upon the
youth and the need for rejuvenating the juvenile department,
the creation of a detention home, a more responsible handling
of juvenile cases, and a stepped-up preventive program in the
churches, schools, and community agencies.

Racial, cultural, youth, and aged needs in the community
afford the alert minister the opportunity for needed courageous
leadership.

Seasonal Decorations and Dramas

One church of my particular acquaintance has become known
through a wide area because of its symbolic seasonal decorations. It all began with the creativeness of the minister who en-
listed and organized the talent of the church and city.

Nearly every one of the famous Easter and Nativity pageants across America had its beginning with a minister who was alert to unusual possibilities.

The slogan of a contemporary corporation could well be the minister's: "The future belongs to those who see it before it arrives."

LETTER WRITING

A pastor said to his friend, "I just don't have the time to keep up with my personal correspondence." Like most ministers, he was busy with the multitudinous duties of his pastorate. However, time spent by the minister in letter writing will not go by unrewarded and merits the hours required from a busy schedule. Few pastors have ever utilized the full potentials of this aid to their ministry. Personal letters can be a powerful public relations factor.

Dr. George Butters of Boston used to give this formula of success to divinity students: "Pray without ceasing, shave every day, and be prompt in your correspondence." One of the most difficult disciplines is promptly answering letters, and ministers have a notorious reputation for negligence in this regard. A system needs to be devised with a folder for incoming mail, which is processed and answered immediately, then placed in outgoing mail for delivery. An efficient secretary is invaluable to a minister and should take the responsibility of seeing that letters are answered on the very day received, with carbons filed alphabetically. If a letter requires research or referral, then its receipt can be acknowledged until the proper information can be assimilated.

The minister who promptly answers his correspondence indicates to his public that he is well organized, an efficient manager, and is never too busy to give attention to individuals. This is good public relations.

Thank You Notes

Courtesy letters show others that the minister is thoughtful, gracious, and appreciative. One minister of my acquaintance has a wide reputation for sending "thank-you" notes. A job in the church or community is never done without his notice and acknowledgment. If a job is worth asking someone to do, it is worth thanking the person after it is done.

"Thank you" is a powerful phrase. Everybody likes to be thanked. To make a person feel that he is appreciated, that his work really counts, and that someone has noticed his services is to gain his good will.

A basic breach of etiquette indicative of thoughtlessness and selfishness is to fail to express gratitude. Endless opportunities for expressing thanks occur in the church and community as well.

In the church I serve, each Thanksgiving Sunday we have Appreciation Letter Day, when all members of the congregation are encouraged to write thank-you letters to those whom they appreciate. It may be to someone working behind the scenes, or one who is in the public eye and criticized; it may be a teacher or a youth. Letters are collected and dedicated during the worship service and mailed together the next day. The effect of such a program is indescribable. Servants of Christ do not work to be seen or praised of men, but to the glory of the Lord. Nonetheless, we are all sufficiently human to work harder when we feel what we do is appreciated. Unexpected courtesy notes really pay dividends.

The minister might pause to reflect upon the many things he undoubtedly has taken for granted, then ask himself, "How long has it been since I wrote a note of thanks to my staff members? the organist? the custodian? or my wife? Have I expressed appreciation to the church school teachers, ushers, choir members, young people? Have I ever written to the newspaper editor to express my gratitude for the space he gives to church news? [He might faint from shock because usually the only time he hears from ministers is when they are complaining.] Have I ever thought of writing to express appreciation to the police chief? school superintendent? the teachers of my children? or the Lions Club for helping the underprivileged? Have I adequately thanked many public-spirited citizens who are helping to make my city a better place to live?"

When a minister is thoughtful enough to express sincerely his appreciation, it will cement his relations with the civic leaders of his community as nothing else can.

Every week undoubtedly someone in the community or church is honored in some way: a football player who excelled in a game, a lady elected to an office in the P.T.A. or garden club, a layman with his picture in the morning news. The church should subscribe to the daily paper so the minister's secretary can clip the news story and send it, accompanied by a note of congratulation, from the pastor.

Wedding anniversaries, birthdays, bereavement anniversaries, and anniversaries of joining the congregation afford opportunities for a pastoral ministry by mail.

Young people will prize forever a personal, sincere, unexpected letter from the pastor. Congratulations may be sent concerning the youth's leadership, some service he has rendered, his outside activities, or honors that have come his way. The letter need not be long. Just enough to make the youth feel important and that his progress is being followed with interest. The letter will spur him on to greater effort and will tie him closer to the church.

Youth is the time of greatest loss to the church. To sustain the interest of this group and to lend encouragement should be a pastor's major interest, and this can be partially accomplished through timely letters. A minister should be alert for opportunities, for each has a tremendous public relations value with the parents, grandparents and friends of every youth.

CHECKLIST OF COURTESY LETTERS

Welcome

   To new members
   To new people in town
   To new public school teachers
   To visitors at services
   To new ministers
   To business persons
   To city officials

Thank You

   To guest speakers
   To givers of personal gifts
   To givers of special gifts to church
   To ushers
   To greeters
   To organist
   To department chairmen
   To young people giving leadership
   To church-school teachers
   To funeral directors
   To police chief
   To public school administrators
   To newspaper editors
   To public servants

Acknowledging

   Wedding anniversaries
   Baptism
   Birth messages
   Birthday greetings

Outstanding attendance record
Outstanding community work
Bereavement

Congratulations

Upon completing a church course
Upon newly elected office in church or community
Upon honor that has come
To new committee members

Sarcastic Letters

It is usually best not to write letters to persons while in the white heat of anger. If a minister feels he must write a letter to give vent to his emotions, then he should postpone the mailing until he is in a calmer mood when reason, good judgment and objectivity can screen his language. Generally, such letters will be filled with barbs and unconcealed venom; therefore, they should be burned. Wrong impressions and hurt feelings are sure to result, and consequently ill will.

Occasionally, pastors will write indignant protests to the newspaper or magazine editors concerning some issue. In fact, editors agree that some of the most bitter, ill-spirited letters come from ministers. The average reader of such outbursts regards the writers of them as intolerant and narrow-minded cranks. Nasty letters with name calling and dogmatic generalizations hurt the reputation of a minister. Courtesy is always in taste.

A good rule is never to put anything in print with insinuations that reflect upon another's character, or that criticize a position without prayerful and deliberate consideration.

John Ruskin's example is worthy, "I never wrote a private letter to any human being which I would not let a bill-sticker post six feet high on Hyde Park Wall, and stand myself in Piccadilly and say, 'I wrote it!' "

Pouring Oil on Troubled Waters

John Timothy Stone, one-time president of the Presbyterian Theological Seminary, said, "In almost all churches there are those members who for one reason or another are out of sympathy with the church, and who do not hesitate to express ill will or grievance when the opportunity affords."

By virtue of his position, the minister usually falls heir to answering the grievances. Often letter writing can be utilized in "pouring oil on troubled waters."

Several principles must be kept clearly in mind. First, the complaint should be promptly answered. If one cannot give a definite decision immediately, he can write a brief note expressing regret for the cause of the complaint and assuring the person that prompt action will be taken.

The opening paragraph is to get in step with the reader. This may be done by thanking him for his inquiry or utterance, expressing regret for the occurrence, assuring him that the difficulty will be corrected, or using some other point on which the writer can agree with him. Such an opening disarms the reader and puts him in a receptive mood.

The writer should indicate to the reader that his point of view is appreciated, and avoid using phrases such as "I cannot understand," or "I am at a loss to know," "you claim," "you state," "your complaint." These expressions are likely to antagonize him at a time when he is already irritated.

Regardless of who is at fault, one should indicate at the beginning of the letter that he is not averse to receiving complaints and criticisms. Instead, he should show the complainant that he regards his grievance as an opportunity to serve him, and that, whether right or wrong, he will gladly investigate the matter.

The minister should avoid sending letters that show irritation. Rather, it is best for him to be courteous, not sarcastic, to use persuasion not argument, to look to the future not to the past difficulty. He will avoid blaming another member of the staff.

Example:

Dear Mrs. Huckaby:

You will never know how embarrassed I was to discover that we had omitted Betty's name from the list of high school seniors published in last Sunday's bulletin.

Every item of copy is edited carefully and then the proofs are checked. While we try to keep mistakes at a minimum, once in a while some seemingly preventable error occurs. When it does, of course we are anxious to correct it.

Please tell Betty that we are running a correction in next Sunday's bulletin.

Thank you for bringing the matter to my attention.

Cordially yours[1]

CONSIDERING IMPRESSIONS

Arthur Krock in his column in *The New York Times* once wrote that "among the anomalies of the American scene is that public relations is an art which often is comprehended least by those who most depend upon its sound practice."

The minister of the church does depend upon public relations. As a matter of fact, what the public thinks of him and his church, rather than what he thinks of it, gauges the success or failure of the enterprise. To many people, the minister is the personification of the institution he represents. He is the image of the church. Therefore, his personal character, his spiritual qualities, the initial impressions he makes are extremely important.

Every minister needs to have an inward look and reflect upon his image of the ministry and contrast that with the impressions he is making. "What is the image I give of the ministry? Do I give the impression of being a man of God? Do I emanate confidence so that people believe I have a sure foundation and know the way from personal experience? Do they trust

[1] Harrall, *Successful Letters for Churches*, p. 114.

me with their confidences? Do I make people feel at ease? Do people feel that I am genuinely interested in them as persons? Do people conclude that I am a man of prayer and in contact with the Lord?"

The minister does live in a fish bowl. The way he dresses indicates something of his tastes and character. A minister should dress appropriately for all occasions. Though the people of this modern day have liberalized a great deal in regard to their ideas of dress, when in question it is always prudent to be on the conservative side. The impressions one young minister made were very shocking when he wore Bermuda shorts while conducting a summer worship service in the sanctuary. Such informality has no place in such a setting, and it reflects the sensational, deliberate attempt of liberality on the part of a minister who left the impression he was careless with the sacred, inconsiderate of the scruples of others, and was striving for the unusual. A minister should strive to gain a reputation from the thoroughness of his preparation, the depth of his Christian insight, and the unselfishness of his service.

One's personal manners should reflect the thoughtfulness, kindness, and courtesy of a man of God, whether it be in the office, at the dinner table, or behind the wheel of an automobile. The way he treats his wife and children in public does not go unnoticed. The town's people would rather "see a sermon than hear one any day," so the minister should be kind and considerate with the grocer, the service-station man, and others of the community who serve him. A grouchy, complaining, inconsiderate attitude is most unbecoming to a minister and can easily circumvent his influence.

Even the way the minister's family keeps the lawn, parish home and car reflects his industry, neatness and cleanliness. These may seem quite inconsequential, yet they do leave impressions, either adverse or complimentary.

So many little unconscious things can be misconstrued by church members, especially those hunting for something for which to criticize the minister. It is a mark of mature, astute leadership to consider the impressions that the things one does and says will leave, before doing or saying them.

The minister who flaunts his knowledge, brags about his accomplishments, "toots his own horn," and generally "knows it all" gives the impression of a conceited egotist. If he has written a book, naturally he wants the world to know it, and undoubtedly he is convinced that everyone has been waiting for this product from his pen. Hence, it deserves to be a best seller. Nonetheless, he must be careful not to let this dominate his conversation or to refer "in my latest book . . . I say thus and so." One is reminded of the minister who, wishing to publicize his recent publication, began his Sunday morning invocation with the words, "O Lord, Thou who has also written a book. . . ." In conversations the minister draws other people out, and does not always talk about himself or his ideas.

Again, a minister must be careful about the references he makes to his former parish or community. In the first place, he should make a clean break and not be forever going back to see old friends or perform pastoral functions. This in itself is a breach in ministerial ethics. His vocal references should be few and restrained. "If he liked it so much and that was such a great church and his friends there are so much better, why did he leave, or why doesn't he go back?" is a common reaction. He should not be openly remorseful about coming to his present charge. The decision was made; he made it. He should make the best of the circumstances without complaining about the weather, or treatment, or the parish home. If the parishioners know of his displeasure, they will not feel more kindly, only impatient and irritable.

Often a minister becomes discouraged, and he may have a right to, with the halfhearted support so often received. Nevertheless, he should exercise care not to convey it publicly, or to speak his mind while depressed, or to scold the people present who may not be the ones responsible for lack of support. It is better psychology to be positive, to boost, to compliment, to

praise those who are loyal, and to work constructively and objectively at the situation that is irritating.

When gifts are given, and they are showered upon ministers
more often than most community personages, a minister must
be careful to be joyously thankful and humble. Such remem-
brances are voluntary expressions of love. Gifts are not upon
merit. A minister has an obligation to be appreciative and over-
joyed with whatever is given, because it is out of overflowing
hearts of love, as a gesture of affection and thoughtfulness.
Perhaps he should humble himself by asking, "Why me? What
have I done to deserve such friendship? Have I been thoughtful and unselfish?" Remember the admonition of the Lord, "It
is more blessed to give than to receive."

"The minister gets along so well with his staff. He seems to
love every one of them." This is a real compliment, and yet it
should be so with Christian co-workers. Congenial, happy staff
relations are difficult, however, for two reasons. First, because
congregations often do not know how to work with a multiple
staff. People find it difficult to give equal allegiance and loyalty
to more than one minister. Constantly they draw comparisons,
make derogatory insinuations, drive wedges, and fail to respect
job descriptions. Secondly, personalities do not jibe easily.
Even the most sanctified find subtle jealousies creeping into
relationships because of encroachment into one's own job ter-
ritory, or the popularity of a co-worker, or the "lying down on
the job" of another. Though an administrator has to insist upon
fulfillment of work and adherence to a job description, yet a
minister must learn to utilize the popularity of his staff members. They are not in competition; they are members of a team.
Therefore, he should not be afraid to compliment privately and
publicly his co-workers, nor to give the credit and attention
while he takes a "back seat" occasionally. To maintain rapport
with one's staff and not to be aloof and unapproachable is essential.

A minister's attitude toward his predecessors is important,
for each one will still have a loyal following within the congre-

gation. In fact, some predecessors may find it difficult to break relations, or some members of the congregation may find it difficult to transfer loyalty to a successor. Some may even resent a new minister's coming and continue to call back a former minister for weddings and funerals. To be sure, the former minister, if he adheres to a ministerial code of ethics, will not come back to a former parish except under unusual circumstances, and then only to assist the present pastor by his invitation. Whatever the circumstance, and however one may feel personally about his predecessor, he must not talk derogatorily to anyone about him, nor be cool to him, nor publicly show resentment. This may be especially difficult for the minister's wife. She may flare in anger and reveal to a confidant or the entire congregation her jealousy. It is best to utilize the former minister's popularity, to be appreciative openly of his accomplishments, and to compliment him. The congregation, if it has any judgment, will feel increasingly his encroachment if he returns too often, and will feel he is not its rightful minister. However, it will resent criticism by the present minister and will defend the one being attacked.

A minister should work just as hard and devotedly as the laymen of his church. There is no place in the ministry for a lazy pastor. If done conscientiously, there is more work than there are hours to do it. The study required for adequate preparation of sermons and teaching is a full-time job alone. The administration of a church in this complex, "go-getter," modern world consumes too great a majority of the minister's time, and then can be done only partially. Pastoral counseling and visitation could well consume every hour of every day. It is a frustrating experience—three full-time jobs usually in one portfolio within the limits of a day. A minister should never be accused of not doing his job because of loitering or wasting time, or skimping on the job. He must choose what is most important, and not consume his time in trivialities. This is where great ministers can be separated from the mediocre. It needs to be said that he will work better, more refreshed, with finer spirit—and live longer, by the way—if he takes one day off per week for diversion. His congregation will willingly concede this time for recreation.

How the minister manages his personal financial affairs has public relations value. He needs to be careful that he does not give the impression that he is greedy. To maintain his financial integrity within the community, he must live within the limits of his income and pay his bills when due. Usually this will require a simple standard of material desires, an understanding, sacrificial family, and prudent frugal spending by both the wife and husband. Congregations are more and more coming to realize the costs of living and are gradually lifting the salary scale to relieve the minister's family from the necessity of living a bare existence.

A minister should not be a "money lover," but he does have to live. To the congregation's shame and blame, too often he has been unable to pay his bills or provide adequately for his retirement. Tortured by fears, ministers quite understandably have sometimes evidenced what looked like unreasonable concern for more income. They have worked on the side, dealt in real estate, traded automobiles, done odd jobs, played the stock market, all of which has diverted their energy from their main job. A minister has as much right to make wise investments as anyone else, as long as they be honest and upright. However, care should be taken that they not absorb his major interest or time. Too, it may be better to invest through his denomination's channels where perhaps a smaller but surer return is realized, and so that local brokers do not know his private business.

Generally, however, a minister should patronize local business people. To buy a car in a neighboring city is a knock at the community where he serves and receives his income. The reasons which cause a minister to encourage people to belong to the church where they live should cause a minister to patronize businesses where he lives. One should be careful about purchasing "foreign products" rather than American products for the same reason. Frequently, businessmen give the minister a "professional discount." Such courtesy can be accepted with graciousness; however, it should never be solicited nor expected.

A minister must learn to take criticism and to make every knock a boost. Not even the noblest of God's servants escape the barbs of the human spirit, Jesus Christ notwithstanding. The minister should not become defensive when attacked. Rather, he should leave the impression that he welcomes constructive criticism, is not adverse to receiving complaints, and is conscientious in striving to render better service. He can learn from criticism if he will honestly examine himself to see wherein there might be a basis for the complaint.

The modern minister with God's agony for the world on his heart, does not have the time to coddle all the disgruntled and proverbial "gripers." When criticized severely, however, it may be prudent for him to talk face to face with the complainant. In such an interview the minister must exercise control of temper, demonstrate a large-heartedness, and be thoughtfully and patiently Christian.

He may say something like this: "Mr. Smith, I understand that you object to something that I have said (or done, or the program being launched). Is that right?"

"Yes, pastor, that is right." (Let him enlarge.)

"Mr. Smith, admittedly, I make many mistakes, but I never intentionally offend anyone. When I do, I am sorry. Now, I respect your judgment. Perhaps you have not understood the point I was making" ("or the program projected").

"Oh, yes. I understand it thoroughly."

"I need your counsel, Mr. Smith. How would you suggest we proceed?" (Or, "How would you suggest it be said?" or "What do you think is the Christian approach?")

This type of approach will mellow and oftentimes remove the barrier. Misinformation is so often the cause of criticism. By humbly seeking the counsel of the complainant, one may win his cooperation.

MAKING THE RIGHT CALLS

The era of the "country parson" who visited repeatedly in every home of his parish is perhaps over. We do not expect the modern physician to call upon us at our homes as the old-fashioned family doctor used to do. Distances are too great and time too short for him to see all of his many patients in this manner, so we go to his office for our examinations and therapy.

Just so should be the church members' consideration of their pastor. In this complex, busy, scattered, modern society it is quite possible for a pastor to drive to the extremities of a large city in an afternoon, stop to call upon two dozen of his members' homes, and find no one there. This is no exaggeration. During the same hours, several persons seeking counseling might drop by his office. The modern minister's time which used to be given to routine home visitation is being absorbed increasingly in counseling.

Nevertheless, the minister does need to be faithful in making the right calls. He must choose wisely and carefully, yet impartially, those upon whom he calls, so that he meets human needs. Nothing will so gain the confidence, esteem, and love of the congregation, and through them the entire community, as the pastor's prompt calling upon the sick, the bereaved, those in trouble, and the shut-ins. Contrariwise, nothing is so damaging to his influence as to be careless and negligent at a time when he is needed and wanted. Routine calls at the hospital at least twice each week are paramount in importance because people are most susceptible to spiritual values at the time of sickness, the birth of a child, or the death of a loved one.

A minister should systematically call in the homes of the officers of the church and the church-school teachers. He may have to do this in the evenings when the families are together, but such calls are "right" and necessary.

One technique which I use in meeting the membership of a rather large congregation is to divide it into small neighborhood groups. Then I spend one night each year in a particular neighborhood when I invite all the families by mail to meet me at a particular pre-arranged home. The evening is a "come and go" affair, essentially social, but it does afford a semi-personal call, and opens doors for offering pastoral counseling assistance to those who may wish to come to my office.

Increasingly, there is emerging in practice the New Testament and Protestant concept of "the universal priesthood of believers," in which every member assumes the role of a minister. This means that every person is an evangelist and has pastoral responsibilities for others. Certainly in the area of evangelism and spiritual oversight the lay folk must assume more and more responsibility. Hence an organization of week-by-week lay visitation is imperative in the modern church. The average pastor cannot do it all.

Nevertheless, the pastor should do some regular, week-by-week personal evangelistic visitation himself. My particular denomination is recommending that one night each week the pastor take a different layman with him to call upon prospective members. The late Dr. P. H. Welsheimer, who ministered for over forty years in Canton, Ohio, made it a rule to make five evangelistic calls every day. Little wonder his congregation grew to such enormous proportions.

Other "right" calls which a pastor needs to make are upon new members, newlyweds, new parents, key persons of influence who may not be on the board, persons in destitution, men in their businesses, newspaper editors, religious editor, school superintendent, TV and radio program directors, hospital administrators, funeral directors, Y.M.C.A. and Y.W.C.A. directors, community welfare directors, the mayor, Chamber of Commerce secretary, juvenile judges, and so forth. Whenever the pastor goes into a place of business, however remote, small or large, he should identify himself. Such a visit will be remembered and may open doors for future ministry.

Use the Telephone

Increasingly in this day when people are difficult to find at home and when most every home and business possesses at least one telephone, the minister can use this medium to a great pastoral advantage. A few hours per week telephoning members and prospects perhaps can benefit more than home visitation, especially so in a large city where distances are great and homes widely scattered. Usually it costs no more to use the telephone for a hundred calls than for a single call, so the church should get its money's worth out of this blessing of science.

One minister telephones all the visitors who attend the Sunday's service, expressing his personal interest in them. Often such a conversation leads to discussion about membership or pastoral counseling needs.

Dial-a-Prayer

One of the most beneficial spiritual services that can be rendered to a community by the church is a daily "dial-a-prayer." The minister dictates daily a one-minute personal prayer which, if done well, will meet the needs of many in the community. For this to be a lasting and effective service, it will require special equipment from the telephone company and at least two extra lines beyond the present telephone system. The "electronic secretary" machines which are used for typical answering services are not designed to take the heavy traffic that such a service will attract.

The advantage of this service is that people of all denominations and those of no affiliation will begin to use the dial-a-prayer with regularity. Therefore, the service and not the sponsoring church needs to be promoted most. The minister, if he is conscientious in this service, will find it confining, but rewarding.

Occasionally, one hears a minister rebel at these general suggestions saying, "I am not concerned about what people think of me or my church."

This is unfortunate. Every parish minister, to be the most effective servant of Christ, must cultivate a favorable public opinion. He must develop the best possible impression as God's man.

This is more than publicity technique, or supersalesmanship, or emergency procedure. It is the entire method of operation by which the public becomes better and more favorably acquainted with the minister and the church he serves.

By careful evaluation and improvement of these exposures, the minister has a better opportunity to win souls for Christ.

Broadcasting Religion

CLIFTON E. MOORE

MANY PEOPLE HAVE GONE west to find gold. I didn't. I made the treck to California to discover new ways to tell an old story. Eleven years and two pastorates after I was graduated from the Theological Seminary in Princeton, New Jersey, I hitched a ride with a friend from Cleveland, Ohio, to Los Angeles, California, leaving my wife and our two children, eight and ten, to tidy up, sell a household of furniture, finish a term of school and drive our eight-year-old Ford west to meet me later. I had a date with the National Broadcasting Company. It was a six-week institute to which I had been admitted.

"It takes a lot of guts to give up a successful six-year pastorate in Cleveland for such a wild goose chase as you're on," observed my physician friend as we waited one day in the hot Arizona sun for a tire to be changed. I knew, however, that he was in sympathy with my cause for he had observed that the church is often directing all its efforts toward reaching the reached—preaching to the converted.

Might I drop the story right there except to say, we did get the tire fixed, we arrived in Los Angeles, I completed the NBC Institute and am now looking back over nearly thirteen years of a ministry in Radio and Television. Part of the time I served as a minister in this field for a 6,000-member church, but more of that time in the dual capacity of Radio-Television Director for the Los Angeles Presbytery.

What experiences and observations I pass on in these pages are my own. I am not writing for or in any way committing the above organizations. It is an interesting position from which to reflect, for as far as I know, I was the first Protestant clergyman to devote full time in production of religious programs in any American city.

Several years ago we conducted a survey in Los Angeles and found that more than three hundred programs of a religious nature were heard or seen on radio or television each week. The overwhelming preponderance of these were created to reach the reached. Hymns, prayers, Bible readings and sermons were employed on almost all of them, each with the same minister holding forth weekly. It was quite all right to observe these facts and praise God that we were so fortunate as to have so many "churches of the air." However, there was one damaging fact revealed. The audience for these programs was miserably low. Most of them had an 0.3-rating, which means that the body is scarcely warm any longer. The churches or the clergymen purchased the air time on the premise that they were reaching a large audience out there in "radioland." The $300 the church might have paid for time each week could have been handled more judiciously and with greater reliability for "the Lord."

A case in point is KFAC in Los Angeles. A fine, respected station broadcasting classical music refuses to sell or to give time for worship services of the air. The station found it difficult to sell the time after such broadcasts for an hour or more following their terminations. Strategywise, one or two such programs might have built a respectable audience among the shut-ins and the indigent church members, but not 275 worship programs a week with 275 sermons.

Perhaps this is a good place to ask the question, "Who is your audience?" The audience is men and women of all ages and stages of affluence. Some are of humble origin and of bare economic conditions. Many are intellectual and educated, many are not. In that vague mysterious audience are children and teen-agers as well. To broadcast to that audience summons as much courage as is required to walk a cable stretched across the Niagara gorge. However, it can be done.

It would be more to the point to inquire, "What is the mood or temperament of your audience?" Many who are listening to the radio may be driving a car, preparing breakfast, having lunch, cleaning the house, or painting a boat. Let it be remembered that only a small fraction of your listeners are giving you undivided attention. Therefore, your message must be tight. Tell them what you are going to tell them in your first sentence. "Today I shall talk with you for five minutes about one word —that word is 'Forgiveness.'" In the second sentence you define the specific type of forgiveness. Then you stay on that subject to the end. Remember that the listener may get out of his chair and go to the refrigerator for something to eat while you are in the midst of your message. You should write so that the interruption is not fatal. You must force yourself to recognize how entirely different the receptivity of your audience in broadcasting is as over and against the rapt attention you think you have at 11:00 o'clock on Sunday morning.

Several years ago a businessman traveling from Kansas City to New York found himself next to an interesting, well-read man whose conversation was most stimulating. After an hour or so in the club car, he invited the stranger to share a drink, which he graciously refused. Then he asked his name, and was somewhat surprised that he gave only a first name. Laughingly, he refused to identify his occupation, explaining that the businessman might get up and leave. The following Sunday in New York he followed up on an invitation to meet the stranger at a certain address in Manhattan. To his amazement, he found the stranger to be the pastor of one of New York's most frequented churches.

Following the service, the two men met in the office of the cleric. As a result the clergyman was asked to aid the businessman in a problem he had with alcohol. Today the latter is an active member and generous supporter of a church in Kansas City. Recently he confessed to me that he would not be in the church today, in all probability had he known his traveling companion was a minister. "I would have found some excuse to move elsewhere that day on the train. I was afraid of preachers then." I asked him why, and his explanation is noteworthy

—"I had never attended church up to that time and the only knowledge I had of the Protestant clergy was through the radio; occasionally I heard a sermon on the air."

This leads us to inquire about the image our Protestant clergymen have created and are creating. The broadcasting industry is capable of creating a public image. The image of the Protestant clergy is somewhat tawdry and this industry is partially responsible for it. The responsibility for this does not rest with the broadcaster so much as with the people who have been doing the broadcasting for us. Here are some of the reasons for this unfortunate image:

1. Religious broadcasting is synonymous with a church service competing with itself.

2. The only time a Protestant cleric is seen or heard on the air, his finger is pointed at you in a sermon. He should be seen as a human being in other roles.

3. Clergymen have used broadcasting to build large congregations they serve and have not been mindful of the total strategy of broadcasting. The cause of all churches should be considered, as well as effective methods of broadcasting to the unchurched who will not listen to radio or television sermons.

4. The unfortunate solicitation of money over the air has cheapened the picture of the Protestant broadcaster.

5. The charlatans, and we pray God they are small in number, have used broadcasting of religion as a lucrative source of income with little or no concern for the unfortunate image they are creating.

6. The failure of the Protestant clergy to work together in a unified, ecumenical effort.

The Roman Catholic Church in America has created a better image of its priests through broadcasting, since it has not practiced the above so repeatedly.

In the following pages we shall see how the unattractive picture of the Protestant clergymen in the minds of so many might be replaced by using the tools and techniques the modern broadcaster has to pass on to the modern cleric. This certainly is one of the reasons for broadcasting—to create a better image. However, a better image is not merely good public relations—there is certainly more to it than that. The main reason for broadcasting is to fulfill the great commission, "Go preach . . ." and people are in need of the substantial message of Christ perhaps as never before. However, there are many formats in which the modern clergyman can present his ideas. Radio and television can be two strong arms of the church today. Thus, they should be known well and wisely employed. Goals and objectives must be clearly understood before the churchman is ready to proceed to broadcast. Let me list them as I see them:

1. To motivate people to want to join some church and then to serve actively within Christian fellowship in some capacity.
2. To influence dissident members to return to active attendance and to seek some area in which to help the church program.
3. To inspire people to respond to Christian teachings.
4. To help others discover richer value for living.
5. To demonstrate interest in the good of the total community, nation and world.
6. To teach the response of Christian love, understanding and forgiveness wherever possible in life's situations.
7. To inspire people to love God unceasingly and to identify with Christ in the problems of everyday living.

If these and other objectives are before you as you anticipate your broadcasting efforts, your motives will be pure and true to your high calling. God looks with pity and disfavor upon any other than high and holy purpose. The media are too powerful and influential to be exploited by inferior motives by men of God. Shun the following motives:

1. To gain prestige. The clergyman who has lost his humility is as a withered vine.
2. To build up your own church without building all churches in the community at the same time.

3. To make money. Money can be made in religious broadcasting. One defrocked clergyman bought fifteen minutes a day five days a week in a certain Eastern city and at the end of his first year he cleared thirty-five thousand dollars.

4. To seek an advancement. Occasionally the pulpit is not used so much as God's footstool as the preacher's steppingstone. To the sincere clergyman the same figure of speech applies to the microphone as to the pulpit. Let your motives be high and God will certainly bless you.

The Federal government requires that a certain amount of Public Service time be granted to community projects. In a city of a hundred thousand people, you probably have one television station to service that city and the surrounding community within a radius of fifty to sixty miles. There are, let's say, two radio stations. There are some forty Protestant churches within this broadcasting area. If you approach the program director for free (or Public Service) time for just your church week-by-week, and if he grants your request, you can imagine the problem he has created for himself. The clergymen of various denominations will likely ask for similar time. Therefore, while he may fulfill your request, the possibility is remote.

Your second alternative is to buy the time from a station. This will eliminate some of the churches or denominations who can't afford the purchase. The manager of the station still has a problem with others who may be inspired by your success on the air. Is he to sell time to all of these clergymen and present a solid block of religious programming from 11 A.M. to 5 P.M. each Sunday? If he does this, he must sell time to the Roman Catholics and the Jews, to say nothing of the many independent groups which circulate teletapes and radio transcriptions all over the country through a syndication manager.

While I would not discourage the above approach, rather I would suggest a method that would solve the problem for all concerned. In a city of this size you might invite five or six Protestant clergymen, whom you deem to be interested in such a project, to a luncheon to discuss a radio and television ministry in your city. Set up this meeting with the knowledge of the president of the local ministerial association. As you proceed, you will find other clergymen who will express a desire to serve with you. I would also incude the more conservative clergymen who are not necessarily in a Council of Churches organization, i.e. Southern Baptist, Missouri Synod Lutheran and the Adventists. Their presence strengthens your position with the station. This first meeting must be exploratory and deal only with the desire to work together and not with formats and participants.

The next step is to make an appointment with the program director at the station and call on him as a group. Express to him your desire to work as a group and to have free time (Public Service time), offering in return promotion and advertising of your new program. We shall touch on the "how" of promotion later.

The likelihood is that the director will grant your request. Do not expect a "good" time at the outset. At first he will sound you out to see if your group can produce, and next he will check carefully to ascertain the size of your audience.

This happened to me with Channel 13, KCOP, in Los Angeles. Initially I was given 4:00 to 4:30 P.M. on Friday for a panel program which we call "The Press and the Clergy." The station advised me to select clergymen who could ad lib answers to questions put to them by people from the press. "No prepared questions, no prepared answers," were the station directives: "Select clergymen who can think on their feet and select subjects in which the total community might have an interest." After six months we were moved to 5:00 P.M. on Sunday. A year later the program was set at 6:30 P.M. each Sunday. Finally we had arrived. We were on the air in the number two market in the country at a prime air time, and "the show" was a "sustainer." This success was attained by starting slowly and moving up as we merited promotion to better air time. We have always attempted to maintain good station relations. The best tip at this point is to put yourself in the position of the program director and try to see things from his point of view. Knowing some of the problems he faces as a broadcaster will help you do this.

Spade work is important. Before you arrive for your initial appointment with the program director at the station, acquaint yourself with all programs he airs throughout the entire week. I would attempt to know as much as possible about the programming his competitors are putting on the air. Certainly you should have knowledge of the current religious broadcasting when you make that initial visit. All of this information will be of real value to you when you call on the program director for your second visit, which will be to discuss format.

You must decide in what form or format you will convey your message. Several factors will dictate the right one, the station's suggestion, your budget, amount of time available for production, the intended audience, the over-all strategy for the entire area, your creative urges or the lack of these and others.

To most ministers the first thing that comes to mind is the sermon method or what some men in the industry call the "talk method." Before we move to other and more effective uses of radio and television, let us consider this.

The shelves of my library contain some sixty volumes of sermons. I have not looked through all of them, but only a few. Not a single one of the sermons I re-checked would hold a large radio or television audience beyond a minute or two. All of the messages begin with a certain quantity of Biblical material and then slowly move to the point of view of the audience. The writers of these expositions assumed that the reader would develop interest in just about the same manner as one catches measles—haphazardly. Many of these sermons were not written for "on the air" use, others were. But, by and large, this is how most radio preaching begins.

A Los Angeles preacher asked me to read his sermon before he preached it on a coast-to-coast network. His message was on

Job, and to have grasped what he had written would have presupposed a substantial quantity of Biblical theology. I wrote on the first page of criticism, "Lose the first two pages, visit a hospital in Los Angeles, go home and write about the suffering you saw, then move old Job into this modern context, and your audience will then identify with you throughout." I don't know that he followed this suggestion. I didn't hear him on the air nor did I ever hear from him again on this matter. I hardly expected a "thank-you" note from him since I had recommended surgery rather than sugar pills.

If you don't *feel* your message, please be advised no one else will either. I've often thought the best time to preach a sermon on immortality is right after you've seen a parishioner die. You might try having your secretary call all your members to come to church that night to hear what you have to say on the subject. If I were one of your flock I would bend every effort to hear you.

If you have any hope of reaching the uncommitted by the preaching technique, you must identify with them where they are, then you and they together take a journey to Bible-land for spiritual insights and wisdom. A writing coach, Helen Hinckley, once said, "You must say to your reader 'Hey, there,' and have him answer back, 'Yes?' " If you don't hear that "yes" in the first page of your radio sermon, you have lost him. He switched the dial. It is at this point that radio and television are deadly cruel. It takes just a simple flick of the wrist for your audience to lose you.

The National Broadcasting Company or the Columbia Broadcasting System would not spend fifty or a hundred thousand dollars on one night-time show if a maximum audience could be reached by paying some versed and learned man five hundred or even a thousand dollars to stand in front of a television camera and talk for an hour. If, however, you do propose to use this method, be not deceived by thinking you have a vast audience. It is not being "on the air" that gives you automatically a large hearing, it is the method you employ that gets them and holds them.

One of the methods most neglected by the church is the spot announcement. Every day there are many station-breaks in which spot announcements are used. One Oklahoma radio station used five hundred spots in one twenty-four-hour period. To be sure they didn't cost much on that station. Yet, not a single church announcement was among that number. Many stations will generously provide spots for the churches in the community.

These must be well written with the purpose you wish to accomplish firmly in mind. It is not advisable to attempt an explanation of the "atonement" or "justification by faith" in a ten-second or even a thirty-second spot. You can, however, advise people of a certain course of action at a certain time, and there is a propitious time for spots. Before Christmas, before Thanksgiving, and even before Easter, or on a Saturday, you might use an attend-the-church-of-your-choice-tomorrow spot.

For television the spot should be visual. One or two cards showing people entering a church will do the job as the announcer reads the ten-second message. Thirty-five millimeter slides may be used just as well on television. In the name of cooperating denominations, the station may provide the spot without charge. Certainly it should not be expected to give or sell go-to-church spots to all churches, or even to all denominations in a community. Were this the practice, there would be an almost endless series of spots before our eyes.

As to the areas to be covered in spots, let this be said: there are many more things to be accomplished than might first be envisioned. Here are just a few suggestions:

1. Take your children to Sunday school—don't send them.
2. Individuals or families should pray daily.
3. Translate the Beatitudes into the language of our day with reminder that these are the laws of Christ.
4. Discuss the many facets of stewardship.
5. Examine the Golden Rule in business ethics, at home, at school, at work, at play.

6. Cheating in examination harms the child and is contrary to God's laws.
7. Discuss Christian responsibility in a free society.
8. Present the Christian's social responsibilities (bond issues, better schools, etc.).
9. Discuss the practice of using God's name in vain.
10. Seek a pastor for private free advice when in trouble.

This list will serve to trigger other ideas in your own mind. Do not minimize the value of a ten- or fifteen-second spot for the work of the church. It is perhaps the least pretentious but nonetheless effective way of letting your voice be heard on radio and television.

For twelve years I have broadcast a fifteen-minute program of world-wide, national and local religious news on Sunday morning over a five-thousand-watt radio station in Los Angeles. People of all walks of life tell me they have heard what I call "Religion in the News" over KFAC, the music station. Many of the listeners are not church related. The cost is marginal since I receive the time free as a Public Service program, thus my only cost is the subscription to two or three religious news services. Local clergymen send in announcements of interesting events in their own churches. With the use of an Ampex 600 I pre-record the news on Friday morning, take the tape to the station at my convenience and am free to be somewhere else when this program is on the air.

In an effort to handle news, the point of view is important. I do not use adjectives to praise the church but rather take an objective position. This position attracts many nonchurch listeners, who wonder why I can be somewhat critical of Protestants in my selection of items, and sometimes praise a Roman Catholic priest or a rabbi for some courageous act. I am sure that a lay person or a nonchurch broadcaster could not say some of the things I am able to say through this program. Scarcely a week passes in which I do not receive several written requests for the material I use on "Religion in the News."

Time-wise I break down the news in this fashion: I give

five minutes to world-wide news, five to national and five to local. Occasionally I will open with an editorial on some important news story. Before the election in 1960 I commented on the Protestant opposition to John Kennedy, a Roman Catholic, running for the office of President of the United States. Not all of my mail was complimentary; nonetheless, I set some of my listeners to thinking about bigotry and tolerance.

Another point to be made is that I am known for my denominational affiliation yet I attempt to be fair toward other groups in the selection of news items for all groups. Here is a hypothetical situation—suppose a Lutheran minister does a fifteen-minute news program each week confining his news to items of that one denomination. How long do you think people of other denominations would listen to him? Not long. The feeling will persist that he is broadcasting only to Lutherans. Your total audience of a given denomination might not be more than 2 per cent or 3 per cent of the entire community. You must ask yourself at the outset, who your intended audience is. This will help direct you in the selection of news items.

If the philosophy back of this effort were to be condensed in a single statement, I would say the purpose of this program is to show that the Christian religion should be interested in the totality of life. Of one fact you can be certain, with a news program you are always sure to have ample material, and you need not be concerned about repeating yourself.

For years a local station in Cleveland refused to grant time to the Protestant cause there, claiming a lack of imagination on the part of the clergy in their selection of format. Then an interview program was submitted and that 50,000-watt station accepted the program and even provided transcription facilities for pre-recording. Bill Veeck, Bob Feller, Don Black (after pitching a no-hit game), all of the Cleveland Indians Baseball Club, were interviewed on this fifteen-minute program entitled, "As I See It." Scarry, captain of the Cleveland Browns football team was another sports figure featured. Senator Robert Taft and Governor Harold Stassen were presented in the midst of a hot political campaign. Psychologists, physicians, teachers, ministers, visiting dignitaries from out of town and judges all found their way to WTAM's microphone to be interviewed by a clergyman.

In an interview program of this nature, the object is to show some facets of an interesting life and to show well along in the program that there is a Christian orientation in that life. It is not an interview for the sake of the interview, but to expose the area where that life touches the life of Christ. At times, this can be done in just one or two minutes. Don Black of the Indians conquered his alcohol problem through prayer. This was admitted after he answered questions for ten minutes on how he pitched a no-hitter against the then Philadelphia Athletics.

There is one rule of thumb. Never ask a "yes" or "no" question. Here is a good example: "Did you get a thrill out of pitching a 'no-hitter' in the big leagues?" A bad question. Your guest has only one word to answer, "Yes." The interviewer must make the interviewee shine. So often the converse is true. A better question is: "How did you feel after that last out in your 'no-hitter' last week, Don?" This question affords your guest an opportunity to give an essay answer and brings out more of the information your listener is anxious to hear.

Earlier I mentioned a panel program we have in Los Angeles which I was asked by the station to moderate in spite of the fact that I had no experience as a television moderator. "You learn by doing," the station executive advised. "Just keep the show on the road and protect the interests of all panelists." The first time on the air I was about as graceful as an elephant caught in a revolving door. Making sure that each panelist receives his fair share of participation is far from easy. Occasionally, it means interrupting someone in the midst of a sentence. For some time I had tried to wait until a sentence had been ended before cutting in on a long-winded panelist. Then I discovered that some people are exceedingly clever. They will end a sentence, then say "However" or "Furthermore," before pausing to take a breath. With this technique a guest can go on with a "that-reminds-me-of-a-story" approach for several minutes.

Here are some of the points to keep in mind as a moderator or as a panelist in broadcasting:

1. Keep your question as brief as possible. Don't make a long statement before you ask the question.
2. Make your answer not more than five or six sentences.
3. Cut in on someone when you wish to take exception to what has been said. It is not Emily Post's idea of good manners; however, it is good in a panel since it shows interest and animation. Nothing is as deadly as a slow-moving panel. On the other hand, a good panel is one of the most exciting and interesting forms of radio and television.
4. Select interesting people who are masters of ad lib.
5. Use topics which the whole community is interested in hearing discussed.
6. Do not attempt to rig a panel just for the sake of conflict. Where you have interesting subjects, you should invite people who have differing views. The night before the Oscar presentations I invited Richard Brooks, whose film "Elmer Gantry" was up for five Oscars, to discuss the film with Methodist Bishop Gerald Kennedy, Dean Leonidas Contos of the St. Sophia Greek Orthodox Cathedral, and Dick Williams of the Los Angeles *Mirror*. This was one of the most successful panels I have ever moderated. The conflict was natural and timing was right. The next night Brooks' picture won three Oscars.
7. Warm up some before air time but not too much. It takes experience to know when you have warmed up enough. I have seen more than one good panel program lost before we went on the air.
8. Use name cards for panelists wherever possible.
9. Sit before a table rather than with full legs exposed. Few panelists are good actors and know how to sit properly and yet be in a relaxed position.

10. Be very careful in summary statement if you are a moderator. Usually it is better to ask one or two panelists to summarize in a sentence or two.

There is almost an endless number of subjects to be discussed, and don't hesitate to invite people who are not related to the church to take part in your panels. "Why I don't go to church" would be an excellent subject for such people to talk over with two clergymen on a panel.

Many clergymen have helped to create new images of those in their profession by their activities in specialized fields. These people of the cloth are working in mental hospitals, penal institutions, community centers, counseling offices, church administration and many other rather new fields of service. We presented a thirteen-week series on KABC-TV in Los Angeles on "Target: Alcoholism," with Dr. Howard Clinebell, a Methodist minister, as moderator. He is nationally known for his work in the field and competent to hold his own with other authorities. We invited experts to sit with him in the panel section which followed a five-minute dramatization of some facet of the problem. We estimated a 300,000 audience for the series and were able to help many people with their alcoholic problems.

This half-hour series at 3:30 P.M. Sundays was just as effective as the one which preceded it on the same station, "The Experts Talk Back." We used Dr. Glenn Whitlock, a Presbyterian cleric with a Ph.D. in counseling. The emphasis on this series was to show the clergymen as men willing and able to help people who were mentally troubled or disturbed. We aimed to show that the clergyman was a person to whom one could turn with confidence in a time of deep trouble.

Suffice it to say, the panel format is one that can be most effective in your work in the church. Very small communities do not have a variety of people who might be called upon, yet an effective job can be done with the panel. First survey for yourself the talent potential before you approach the radio or television station.

We have had real success on three occasions with a format known as the "Variety" format. This calls for a general mixture of several things. For an entire year at 7:00 P.M. on Sundays on KTTV we did a program entitled "Within These Portals." We used well-known soloists such as Connie Haines, men's quartets, larger singing groups, a short dramatic segment and Dr. Louis Evans, then minister of the Hollywood Presbyterian Church, in a counseling role and in a concluding three-minute talk on some Christian theme. Many of Hollywood's familiar personalities took part such as Hugh O'Brien, Dennis Morgan, George Chandler of the "Lassie" series, and others.

KRLA is a 50,000-watt radio station that employs disc jockeys day and night. We are on the air 8:30 to 9:00 A.M. and repeat the transcription 11:00 to 11:30 P.M. on Sunday with a program entitled "Spirit of Today." Young clergymen are invited to be the hosts. The format calls for favorite hymns and anthems with commentary, and popular music with commentary. Interviews with students, adults, visiting dignitaries, clergymen and specialists in various fields are presented by the hosts.

We have found that a sense of humor is most valuable on the part of a minister when he is broadcasting to an audience of high school or college youngsters. Recently the Rev. Hugh Nelson of Pasadena did a splendid job of interviewing a clergyman from South Africa, using humor in covering material filled with emotion and differences of opinion. This Variety program requires a different approach than "Within These Portals," but both are Variety shows.

"Faith of Our Children" on KRCA, the NBC station in Los Angeles, is another example of the Variety format put to good use. Our target audience here was children up to the age of thirteen, as well as their parents. We invited the well-known dancing star Eleanor Powell, who taught Sunday school in her own church for years, to act as the MC of the series. Children enacted various scenes, read Bible verses, gave prayers, sang in choirs and performed as pantomimists. We used children from various churches and from the professional entertainment industry. For two years Miss Powell provided her talent (without salary) for the weekly series.

Others who rotated in later series were some of Hollywood's bright lights—June Lockhart, Barbara Rush, Dale Evans, Jane Withers, Colleen Townsend Evans, Wanda Hendrix, Nancy Gates, Coleen Gray, Beverly Garland, Joan Vohs, Janet Waldo (Corliss Archer) and others. Yet the so-called stars were not the superior performers necessarily. Linda Leighton, who would not be classed as such, was one of our most effective people. I mention this to indicate that this idea is not confined just to New York and Los Angeles. Every city must have some trained acting talent available to lead in such a series.

Our scripts were written by competent writers in consultation with Christian Education authorities from the Church Federation and various denominations. Some of them were edited by Alice Banner, the wife of Bob Banner, distinguished director of the Dinah Shore and Garry Moore shows. She is a talented writer and donated her services.

After five years this series went off the air, but not until it had motivated many people to give their services to some phase of church work and had won for the station and all of us six coveted Emmys. Many requests to resume this series have been made and already discussion has begun with executives of KRCA to that end.

The purpose of the Variety format in the instance of the church work is to inform and to inspire. The Ed Sullivan Show on CBS is a good example of a Variety program commercially speaking. In the life of the church there is a place for the program at a church supper in the fellowship hall and there certainly is a place for the eleven o'clock worship service Sunday morning. Each has its place, and each is important. Therefore, this format is certainly to be remembered when it comes to programming in radio and television. Much of your success will depend on two people: the producer and the master of ceremonies.

"Worship in the West" is not an outdoor church service amid the cacti in a remote area of Arizona. It is the title of a radio program from 9:00 to 10:00 A.M. on the music station KFAC each Sunday in Los Angeles and in the format which the industry calls a "Music" show. Except for a few minutes of talk by the church people honored each week, religious music of a classical nature is used from the vast library of recordings the station possesses. Well-known choirs, orchestras, soloists and instrumentalists are often heard on this program. In this case the format belongs on KFAC since this station broadcasts classical music to a select Southern California audience. The people who listen to this type of music would respond positively to sacred classical music. At the conclusion of the program we invite the listeners to attend the church of their choice in the area.

Perhaps the most successful use of the music format for religious radio is to be seen in the CBS Sunday morning program from Salt Lake City, Utah, featuring the Mormon Tabernacle Choir and organ, with a short four-minute message by Richard Evans. On the local area a program similar to this can be created where an outstanding singing group exists or can be assembled.

Nine months is a respectable period of time for a television program to exist. Some have continued two, three or even five years. On November 4, 1961, we celebrated ten years of uninterrupted programming on KTTV from 11:00 A.M. to 12:00 noon each Sunday. The series is entitled "Great Churches of the Golden West" and actually presents a Protestant or Orthodox church service from the sanctuary of a church. Various denominations invite us to visit their churches on Sunday and put their worship services on the air.

By category, this type of television would be termed a "Remote." This format calls for an actual on-the-spot instantaneous origination, such as the World Series, the Pasadena Rose Parade, the Inauguration or the Forest Hills Tennis Tournament. Many people have said, "I would like to visit a church of another denomination." We provide that opportunity each Sunday and we continue to hold an audience of appreciable size. One month an audience research company gave us two-thirds of the total number of sets in use when we were on the air. This is considerable, considering the competition from six other television stations at the time.

According to reliable authorities there are in Southern California 150,000 shut-ins who will not leave their homes or hospitals again. Some sixty hospitals use this telecast in some form or another. We reach all denominations by our system of rotation. Were we to confine ourselves to one denomination we would then reach approximately one-seventh of the audience we have now, since there might well be similar telecasts on the other six stations in our city featuring the other six major denominations.

A vast array of letters crossing my desk over the years attests to the new life we have injected into a church by our visit on Sunday. One cleric reported some twenty-five new families in his Sunday school or church attributable to a "Great Churches of the Golden West" telecast. I am convinced that it is the visitation to the many churches in the area that attracts the large number of viewers. The audience would dwindle to a small fraction of what we have now if we were to visit the same church every Sunday with the same choir and minister. This might not be true if the choir were of the magnitude of the Mormon Choir in Salt Lake City or the preacher were as well known or as widely read as Dr. Norman Vincent Peale.

When it comes to deciding what format you will accept for broadcasting religion on television, don't forget the Remote. People enjoy visiting the various churches in the community.

Jack Paar is a detestable nuisance to many a viewer. He has a way of keeping many of us up late at night when we should be in bed. He is a very familiar broadcasting phenomenon. The Jack Paar Show is what the industry calls a "Personality" show. The Jack Benny and Bing Crosby programs are similar in format. These are built around the personality of the principal figure. Every one and every incident within this type of program is constructed around the central figure. Educational television had such a person in Dr. Frank Baxter.

We decided to try this format with the Bible. Several characteristics are necessary before you are in a position to take your personality to the television or radio executive for approval of your idea. The person you choose must have the following characeristics: teachable, communicative, knowledgeable, humble, confident and quick to abandon a bad idea. In addition to these he must have or must be taught the inside of broadcast operation lest he make excessive demands of the station.

Such a person was found in a minister of a church of some two thousand members. He possessed a Ph.D. from Princeton Seminary and had taught eight years in the divinity school before assuming the pastoral ministry. He had every virtue of a successful broadcaster but one. He was not totally committed to television. How could he be, with such a large church making many demands on his time?

Using slides, still pictures, maps, charts and other visual objects, Donald Gard did a bang-up job for nine months on KRCA, the NBC affiliate in Los Angeles, in "living color." We entitled his show "Covenant," and featured various books of the Bible in the series.

Were Dr. Gard available for script conferences, research, press interviews, appearances on various television programs and for full exploitation, we well might have built "Covenant" into one of the most influential programs on television. Pioneering always presents these challenges. The time may well come when such a charming and capable young man can be freed of pastoral responsibilities to be the church's radio and television authority on the Bible in such centers as New York, Chicago, Los Angeles and other cities.

This is one instance where we experimented with the Personality format and we were pleased with what we accomplished. Thousands of written requests came to the station seeking copies of his material. As the series continued on the air we would hope to invite various appropriate people to be on the program with Dr. Gard. Whether you live in a large metropolitan area or a smaller city, this format lends itself equally well to the religious broadcaster.

The same is not entirely true of another format, namely the "Drama." To use a religious drama effectively on television requires professional writers, actors, technicians and directors. In addition, we have found that actors must be paid in keeping with the minimum set down the by Actor's Guild. The church must compete with high-budget dramatic productions that are constantly being presented on radio and television. To put on the air something of inferior quality with amateur actors and writers, instead of enhancing the cause of the church presents a weak image to the nonchurch people whom you hope to reach by dramatic efforts. On a few occasions we have been fortunate to secure such drama groups as the Pasadena Playhouse presenting "John Witherspoon" on the Fourth of July on our "In God We Trust" program over KTLA, Channel 5. Such an effort requires a great amount of time in script conferences, rehearsals, sets, costumes and promotion. The dramatic format is television at its most expensive and exciting level. I do not recommend that the church avoid it, but I do advise that it be done with professional competence.

There is one other broadcasting method which I highly recommend to people who have a gospel to preach by radio and television. The industry calls it the "Documentary." In this method one employs film clips with or without sound, using narration from the studio. In addition, 35-millimeter slides, still pictures mounted on large cards, art work and various illustrative objects may be used. All of these are skillfully woven together by a clergyman who is able to narrate from the studio as these features are integrated into a carefully scripted program. When you take such a show to the studio, be sure to have ample quantities of scripts for director, technical director, floor man, announcer and others. Specific cues must be written into the script as to the length of time each slide, still picture or film clip is to be on camera.

Let me give specific explanation of how the Documentary

method can be employed successfully. Let us suppose you are to take a trip to the Congo. Without too much expense you can rent a 16-millimeter motion picture camera, a camera for taking 35-millimeter still pictures (slides), and if possible a small tape machine (sound) with which you might take interviews of various people you meet along the way. With a certain amount of coaching by competent people before you take your trip, you can do a fairly respectable job of getting material for a television program or even for two or three half-hour shows.

If you check you television log carefully, you will find that all three of the networks, NBC, ABC and CBS, have used Documentaries effectively and have given prime evening time to some of the broadcasts. Should you take a pen and pad and watch several of these Documentaries, using a stop-watch to time various segments, you will derive substantial benefit.

Assuming that you have decided what format you will use to broadcast, now is the time to consider certain facets of soliciting talent. If you are not to be the producer of your show, then you must select someone who can handle the production end of it. The producer must be responsible for everything that happens on a television program. The station operates in this manner. It cannot keep a list of five or six people with whom it can consult on the various facets of a program, therefore one person must be the over-all boss. It goes without saying that the producer must make it perfectly clear to all talent on his show that he is the source of final authority as to what goes on the air. When the entire package which includes script, actors, props, music and the rest are brought into the studio by the producer, his program is then in the hands of the station director. The producer can tell the director how he wants the pictures taken during the half-hour that the television program is on. The director should bend every effort to grant his requests unless they are technically unfeasible. It is up to the director then to assume the responsibility for all talent and what is done during rehearsal and air time. The producer then sits in the position of a consultant and adviser. Be that as it may, the director advises all members of a production as to how they are to perform.

This relationship between producer and director is very important. A clear understanding between the two is always recommended.

Another person who is equally important on any broadcast is the writer. If a Christian writer is not available, it is not always mandatory to secure a writer who has complete sympathy with the Christian cause. Such a person can be advised by the producer as to the aims and objectives desired for the script, or a technical adviser may be appointed by the producer to work with the writer. One re-write should be requested when you first discuss this script with the writer. This procedure is par for the course. After completion of the first draft the writer should sit down with the producer and others in conference before he does the re-write. Let the writer make all changes you desire. I recommend to every clergyman who would broadcast, Robert Gunning's book, *The Technique of Clear Writing,* published by McGraw-Hill Book Co., Inc. Here is a quotation:

One office worker meets another in the hall. "Joe," he says, "if you need more stickers ask us for them."

His message is nine words. They deliver his thought simply and directly. Anyone can understand. What more is there to say?

But let the same man write this message and he fills it with business jargon:

"If the supply of stickers sent you is not sufficient to meet your requirements, apply to this office for additional copies."

The nine words have grown to twenty-one and the sentence has become heavy reading. But it can be tortured still more by twisting the verb forms. This is the way the written message actually appeared in business copy:

"*Should* the supply of stickers sent you *not be sufficient* to meet your requirements, *application should be made* to this office for additional copies."

A message that in simple form required but ten syllables has now grown to thirty-eight.

A word to the wise is sufficient, except to say that it is always helpful to give any radio or television manuscript to someone else for editing or suggested changes.

When it comes to a minister writing his own sermon for radio or television, be it a five-minute meditation or a twenty-five-minute full-length sermon, there is a certain rule of thumb. Writing must always be clear and in language that the masses can understand. One should never hesitate to re-write a sermon with the thought of boiling it down as much as possible and checking it for "hard" or difficult words.

I keep "a book" on actors and actresses to which I am constantly adding names. Professional guidance can always be secured in any community from people in the radio and television industry when it comes to casting a script requiring acting talent.

There is one tip of real value to any clergyman who is using the Talk format for broadcasting, and that is the use of the voice. When a minister speaks from the pulpit, he has a tendency to project and to pontificate. It seems to be an occupational hazard in spite of the fact that large churches use a public address system. Whether on radio or television the use of the voice is very important. Clergymen must be advised that the normal conversational tone is much more effective and modern than the method sometimes employed by the preacher who projects as though he were speaking to a hundred or a thousand people when he's on the air. Keep in mind that you are speaking to one or two people sitting in the home or driving a car and therefore you speak in the tone you would use in normal conversation with these people were you actually in their presence.

As you move to the last stage of your preparation for producing a new series, there is one final decision—the selection of the title for your series. I had the unusual experience of having been offered a half-hour Public Service time on KCOP-TV with only ten days to prepare. Our format called for two clergymen to be interviewed on the air by two members of the press. I had twenty-four hours in which to select a title for this series, as Channel 13 wanted to release it immediately for the television section of the newspapers. I carried a small pad in my pocket and whenever I got an idea I jotted it down. I followed this procedure all day. The next morning I began scratching off hopelessly impossible titles and finally had two remaining. I phoned the head of the station and told him my first and second choices for a title. He agreed with me on the first choice, "The Press and the Clergy."

For a children's series I began reading a hymnal. After going through about 100 hymns I had the title "Faith of Our Children." There are two sources to which one can always turn for titles, namely, the Bible and Shakespeare. Some people who gain their livelihood in the production field have a notebook with a section marked for titles. Each time a striking combination of words occurs to them they enter it in the title section of their workbook.

Let us assume that the stage is set and the production phases of a new program are all completed. Now begins another and equally important aspect—promotion. One method is to offer in a small city the big story to the local newspapers, with glossy photographs accompanying this story. In a city the size of Los Angeles, send out a release to all of the television editors and the religious editors of the large metropolitan dailies. Also, I send a release to the community papers of which there are more than 100 in Southern California. It is very important that your release be prepared in the proper form. I have the feeling that any story more than a page (double-spaced) in length is entirely too long. Follow-up releases will be much shorter than that—perhaps just a paragraph. Here is a sample release which is an announcement of the most recent series that we launched here in Los Angeles:

FROM:
Rev. Clifton E. Moore
Radio and Television Director
1501 Wilshire Boulevard
Los Angeles 17, California
HUbbard 3-3840—HO 3-4677   *FOR IMMEDIATE RELEASE*
                                  PHOTOS ARE AVAILABLE

Beginning April 16th, KNXT (CBS) Channel 2, will carry for thirteen (13) weeks a series entitled "Insight." The series will be on the air from 4:00-4:30 P.M. each Sunday.

"Insight" is a confrontation of some of the principal figures of Christian history. Each week a contemporary clergyman meets face to face one of the important men of church history. Dean Leonidas Contos of the St. Sophia Greek Orthodox Cathedral in Los Angeles sits in as interviewer for the first series. He will confront such people as Peter, Simon The Cyrene, Paul, Athanasius, Augustine, Luther, Calvin, Tyndale, Adoniram Judson, John Wesley, Roger Williams, Kagawa and others.

David Brian portrays "Peter." Some of his acting roles have been, "Mr. District Attorney," "The High and The Mighty," "Untouchables" and three co-starring appearances in Joan Crawford films.

Don De Fore has been secured for the "Roger Williams" segment. Mr. De Fore has starred in some thirty-six (36) pictures and is remembered for his "Thorny" portrayal in the Ozzie and Harriet Nelson show. He has the lead in a new series, "Daddy-O." Recently he starred in "Facts of Life" with Bob Hope.

Rhys Williams as "Paul" is well known in the theatrical field. He appeared opposite Ethel Barrymore in "The Corn Is Green" and Helen Hayes in "Harriet."

Dr. Clifton Moore, Director of Radio and Television of the Los Angeles Presbytery and Coordinator of the Radio-Television-Film Commission of the Southern California Council of Churches is the producer of "Insight."

The series is sponsored by the Radio-Television-Film Commission of the Los Angeles Federation.
032761

If you have the budget for advertising you might buy an ad in a local newspaper or papers. At the same time you should ask the station to provide you with spot announcements of the forthcoming production. By all means don't forget exploitation. By this we mean asking various newspaper columnists to plant a line or two occasionally concerning your series. Ask a TV-Radio feature writer in your community to do a review of your program.

A release should be sent to all clergymen in the community asking them to announce your series in the pulpit, in monthly church papers and weekly church bulletins. Not all of them will oblige, many will. Also it is good to send a release to the national denominational magazines. Occasionally they use a local item of this nature.

Last, but not least, is the house-to-house "throw-aways." Some printer may provide, inexpensively or as a contribution, several thousand hand bills which can be passed out door-to-door by a group of youngsters from Sunday school classes the Saturday before a new series is to be put on the air. This is more easily accomplished in a city of 100,000 than in a metropolitan area such as Chicago.

Any person who is interested in radio and television for the cause of the church will find workshops available. The United Presbyterian Church in the USA has assigned John Groller, competently trained layman with years of experience in commercial broadcasting, to the task of conducting one-day and week-long workshops in broadcasting in the sixteen western states. This is a service of real value. I recommend that any person interested in broadcasting the gospel attend a workshop. Further insight into broadcasting can be obtained by talks with executives in the industry who are willing to share experiences. Producers of successful shows are sources of valuable information as well.

Carry a small notebook in the glove compartment of your car. Some people are most creative when driving alone. When a creative idea pops into your mind, stop and make notes. Later you may find a great idea for a sermon there or even a germ for a new series for radio or television. Make notes concerning new ways of telling the story. Do not say to yourself, This is how we do it at 11:00 o'clock Sunday morning. Keep searching for the new way which has never been tried before.

Hollywood is where I work. I find this a tangled, twisted city of disappointed people, frustrated and failing. Yet I find Hollywood a magnificent place with thousands of creative and gifted people. It is a city placed on a hill which cannot be hid. It has the know-how when it comes to radio and television. I have used scores of the brightest stars in her firmament on programs for Christ and His Church. This city is no different from any other city. There are many people, if not stars, who will gladly give you a hand for such a worthy cause in your town. Don't hesitate to invite them to join you.

Just as I began my work in Los Angeles, I was asked to solemnize the marriage of a young lady whose parents wrote most of the "Andy Hardy" motion pictures. At the wedding party I was confronted by a young actress, Vanessa Brown, who asked, "Where do you preach, Mr. Moore?" To which I replied, "I do not have a church of my own. I am a radio-television producer for the churches." Somewhat in amazement she commented, "A radio minister, how incongruous!"

Today it is not incongruous. In addition to my work in Los Angeles, there is a clergyman in full-time production in San Francisco and a part-time man in San Diego. There are several others in this country. Doubtlessly the number will increase.

I came West thirteen years ago to find new ways to tell an old story. What I have written here out of these years of experience on the production firing line may or may not be familiar to you. Protestantism deserves a better image of itself through the air-lanes. It should be concerned with the total Protestant effort in any community, it should recognize the problems the industry faces in broadcasting and it must seek new and creative ways of proclaiming the gospel. Clergymen should attempt to strike a balance on the air when it comes to the total role they fulfill in their calling. Seek the format that is most practicable and at the same time imaginative, then produce well and promote well.

May God inspire you and bless you in broadcasting religion.

Ever entertained the ambition to test your talents as author . . . newspaper columnist . . . radio or TV voice . . . publicity pivot? Or has experience in any of these areas served only to discourage your further aspirations?

In this unique "how to" anthology, the admirable arts of ministerial public relations and writing for print and broadcast find provocative new depiction as realistic, inviting enterprises indeed!

Expressly compiled for the contemporary pastor who would broaden the influence of his ministry, *Reaching Beyond Your Pulpit* brings together the applicable